WRITING PSYCHOLOGICAL REPORTS

WRITING PSYCHOLOGICAL REPORTS

By

WILLIAM T. MARTIN, M.Ed.

Clinical Psychologist
Jacksonville State Hospital
President
Psychologists and Educators, Inc.
Jacksonville, Illinois

CHARLES C THOMAS • PUBLISHER

Springfield • *Illinois* • *U.S.A.*

Published and Distributed Throughout the World by
CHARLES C THOMAS • PUBLISHER
BANNERSTONE HOUSE
301-327 East Lawrence Avenue, Springfield, Illinois, U.S.A.
NATCHEZ PLANTATION HOUSE
735 North Atlantic Boulevard, Fort Lauderdale, Florida, U.S.A.

With THOMAS BOOKS *careful attention is given to all details of
manufacturing and design. It is the Publisher's desire to present books
that are satisfactory as to their physical qualities and artistic possibilities
and appropriate for their particular use.* THOMAS BOOKS *will be true
to those laws of quality that assure a good name and good will.*

Printed in the United States of America
Q-1

PREFACE

THIS BOOK is focused primarily on the novice writer who has never written a psychological report. The practicing clinician who desires a concise guide for periodic reference will find this volume similarly useful. Educators in need of an instructional aid for teaching report writing in their counseling and clinical curriculums should likewise be able to put these materials to use. The content of this book is designed to act as a chronological, continuous reference guide with course outlines in mind.

The crux of this text is to instruct, refresh, and guide the clinician or student who desires to learn how to write coherent, consistent, and purposeful psychological reports.

The author is deeply indebted to his friends and colleagues who were kind enough to read portions of the manuscript and offer their suggestions, *viz.* Dr. Richard Alumbaugh* and Messrs. John M. Gullo* and Jim Sichlau of the Jacksonville State Hospital. Especial appreciation is shown for the initial encouragement given in this effort by Dr. Daniel Graham, Sul Ross State College, Alpine, Texas. The permission given by Drs. Eugene Laska and Nathan S. Kline of Rockland State Hospital, Orangeburg, New York, and from Dr. Ralph Slovenko of New Orleans, Professor of Law, to quote from their works is likewise appreciated. Further appreciation is shown for the Honeywell Corporation, IBM Corporation, National Computer Systems, and Physician's Record Company who graciously permitted use of their materials and forms in this book.

The views expressed in this work are those of the author's and do not necessarily represent those of either the Jacksonville State Hospital or the Illinois Department of Mental Health.

W. T. M.

---

*No longer at Jacksonville State Hospital.

CONTENTS

Page

Preface v

Chapter

I. INTRODUCTION 3
II. PURPOSES AND CONTENT OF THE REPORT 5
III. ORGANIZATION OF THE REPORT 14
IV. LANGUAGE OF THE REPORT 23
V. GUIDANCE COUNSELORS, CLINICAL PSYCHOLOGISTS, AND REPORTS 30
VI. THE DIAGNOSIS 40
VII. THE SOCIAL HISTORY STATEMENT 52
VIII. THE PSYCHIATRAC EXAMINATION 57
IX. THE INTELLECTUAL EVALUATION 73
X. THE PERSONALITY EVALUATION 81
XI. THE TREATMENT SUMMARY 91
XII. THE COMPREHENSIVE PSYCHOLOGICAL 99
XIII. COMPUTER APPLICATIONS IN PSYCHOLOGICAL REPORTING 118
XIV. LEGAL IMPLICATIONS OF COMMUNICATION, TESTIMONY, AND REPORTING 147
XV. OVERVIEW 170

Bibliography 173

Appendix 177

Index 181

WRITING
PSYCHOLOGICAL
REPORTS

Chapter I

INTRODUCTION

THERE IS probably not one psychology student, intern, school counselor, clinical psychologist, psychiatrist, psychometrist, or social worker who at one time or another has not been confronted with the task of writing some form of a professional report. The types and purposes of these reports are many. Usually a beginning writer discovers, much to his dismay, that there is no clear-cut procedure or magic formula to follow. As a result, much trial and-error learning is involved, and sometimes without adequate personal satisfaction. This is where this text should be useful.

For some reason or another one eventually becomes oriented as to the nature of report writing and then manages to escape without too many scars. Then, the inevitable shock may occur where the newly evolved writer discovers that his organization or department may require reports altogether different from the way he learned. Such is the educative process!

Even though innumerable manuals, textbooks, and reference guides are available for aiding one in scientific and educational writing, few have been published which specifically relate to the writing of psychological reports (Prakken, 1967). Three texts in particular have been written in recent years dealing with the subject of writing psychological reports. Hammond and Allen (1953), Klopfer (1960), and Huber (1961) wrote texts which were especially directed to the clinical setting. None of these seemed to deal with either the school counseling or the computerization realms. In particular, computerized reports are a relatively recent innovation. Other writers have written some guidelines to follow in report writing but as the reports applied to the clinical setting (Foster, 1951; Garfield, *et al.*, 1954; Lodge, 1953; Tallent and Reiss, 1959; and Thorne, 1956). Morrow

(1954) discussed the diagnostic report while Scott (1953) dealt with the area of forensic reports.

Comprehensive and innovative coverage on the subject of report writing in the psychological sciences has been neglected all too long. Undoubtedly, many educators have thrown up their hands in periodic frustration when they were faced with this instructional area. What usually develops is that the professor gives the student a few hints and then abandons him to his own resources. Or, reports written by others are used as examples, with much of the rationale omitted.

In this text no attempt is made to instruct the writer of reports in the administration, scoring, and interpretation of psychometric insruments, as some other writers have apparently done. It is assumed that the reader is already familiar with these operations. Similarly, instructions in the writing of reports in the medical and vocational rehabilitation areas per se have been omitted from the contents of this book—specialized texts are available in these areas. Instructions are given, however, in the use of the evaluation or diagnostic interview. The interview is an important tool to be used when the clinician is unable for some reason or another to administer psychometric measures; and it is the crux of the psychiatric examination report. It is for these reasons that an entire chapter is devoted to the interview. The influence of innovations in computer technology upon psychological reporting and program evaluation is shown in Chapter XIII. Computerization of technical report writing is a new and important era which is gaining much impetus in the psychological sciences, and the conscientious student should add these principles to his clinical orientation.

Finally, a discussion on the legal implications of reporting is presented in Chapter XIV, since this is felt to be an area of great importance to those writing psychological reports.

Chapter II

PURPOSES AND CONTENT OF THE REPORT

No psychological evaluation of a client or patient should be conducted without sufficient reason. Suffice it to say that no report should be written without a purpose, whatever that purpose may be. Both can very well be executed as a routine function, such as for diagnostic screening purposes; or, on special referral of clients. With these basic concepts in mind one is ready to begin thinking about the writing of a psychological report.

Many will find that they have any number of clever and possibly inspirational comments to include in a report prior to the actual writing. However, one may begin to wonder where these significant thoughts disappeared when faced with that task of composing the psychological report. If you happen to be one of those persons who seems to have difficulty in putting your thoughts, observations, interpretations, and conclusions down in writing, you may very well view the report as a foreboding nightmare. It should not be.

Prior to any writing or reporting task one should have the data available from which to compose the report; if insufficient psychometric or other data are available, it may be difficult to do any reporting. But, a well-written report can be achieved from a single item like an interview or test protocol. Quantity does not in itself make a good report.

The report should not under any circumstances be thrown together haphazardly with the intent of getting something down in writing and nothing more. Each report should be viewed as a significant contribution to the client's over-all record; no one would want to do an injustice by furnishing erroneous material for a record. At least, let's hope not. It is far better to be a little late with a report and to have it correct than to set an organizational record for promptness of irrelevant and inaccurate reports.

From time to time one may hope for some "magic formula" by which to prepare a psychological report; unfortunately, there are none in existence. About the time the writer gains insight into the proper procedure for writing a report he soon becomes dismayed to learn that there are inherently as many *types* as there are reporting situations. Of course, one can become skilled in writing a stereotyped communication to fit all occasions. However, one of this type would create many undesirable problems such as the report not being designed to fit the reader. If there has been no communication between the writer and the potential readers, the writer's effort has been to no avail.

Another preliminary consideration to bear in mind before writing any report is that of *confidentiality*. This may appear to be a trite word for professionals; nonetheless, there are those who have no reservations about disclosing information contained in a client's record to lay persons. It cannot be overemphasized that the very nature of the data included in a psychological report *demands* security. Apart from the ethical presuppositions, the legal considerations of exposing confidential material to extraneous persons are many. Information should *never* be released to anyone at random for the intentional or unintentional purpose of enlightening the layman with "juicy" facts and conclusions. Data contained within a psychological report should only be revealed to a fellow professional for psychological consultations; to the intended reader; or a third party, the latter of which a *release of confidential information* is necessary. More will be discussed in Chapter XIV on this subject.

With the foregoing factors in mind one comes to the more basic purposes of the report. The first and most essential function of any transmittal of information is that of *communication*. This is the core of all spoken and written language. Without it, one flounders in symbolic constructs. The psychological report is a written account of all first-hand data, inclusive of interviews, test results, and the like. At times, certain second-hand information such as the social history may be included in a report (the social history is viewed as first-hand information by the social worker). In this process of communication it is the job of the clinician to ingest all of the factual data surrounding a given client, then intellectually digest it, and finally produce an assemblage of orderly, coherent, and relevant material. The report is considered to be a detailed, but concise, account of the patient's status as of the writing of the report. It is an intertwining of the past, present, and future.

The report should be written so that any intended reader will have no difficulty in understanding its content. More specifically, it should be constructed so as to not insult or to surpass the reader's intelligence. Write the report with the average intellectual level in mind, inasmuch as most of your readers will have average intelligence.

Another primary consideration is that of for *whom* is the report intended? There are usually two types of readers. First, there is the *primary* reader; and, second, the *secondary* reader. The primary reader is any given individual, named or unnamed, who is specifically concerned with the client. Secondary readers include any other readers who may also benefit from knowledge of the client's behavior. An example of a primary reader is the psychologist to whom a counselor is sending a report on a client, in terms of the public or private school setting. The client's classroom teacher may be the secondary reader.

From the clinical standpoint, the primary reader may be the staffing committee and a secondary reader would be any person authorized to read the report in the patient's medical record folder. In a social history report, the writer may be a case worker, the primary reader might be the psychologist. These three situations are by far not the only instances of primary and secondary readers. The possible combinations of primary and secondary readers are virtually limitless. Moreover, the report contents should be communicated so that each type of reader can understand it without difficulty.

Essentially every type of psychological report, irrespective of its potential reading audience, should include certain information. Specific identifying data, psychometric results, sociopsychological observations, interpretive statements, a summary (optional), conclusions (optional), a diagnosis, prognosis, recommendations, and precautions (where applicable) are the usual items in psychological reports. Additionally, there should be some comment made in the report concerning the patient's physical condition as observed by the clinician. These facts and interpretations inform the reader of the past and present status of the patient, the clinician's interpretation of the facts, and certain other information. Irrespective of report formats, styles, organizations, or specific purposes and readers, all reports should include the aforementioned points.

The mere listing of facts and nothing else, reduces the role of the clinician to a record-taker. The use of professional interpretations without the use of background facts creates the image that the clinician was theorizing and little more. All pertinent portions of the report should be present for it to be of optimal value to the reader. If the reader only sees "facts" then, in effect, he must interpret the data himself. Without any doubt, however, most readers *do* seem to interpret report contents to conform to their own theoretical framework—some readers do not. At any rate, the report writer should be responsible for offering the reader *some* interpretations and conclusions as some readers tend to rely on the clinician's interpretations.

TYPES OF REPORTS

Even though the types will be discussed individually in later chapters, they will be briefly mentioned here. The *social history statement* is primarily thought of as the accumulation of facts relating to the patient's home, family, and employment environment prior to and concurrent with his hospitalization. In the case of an out-patient, those facts in the client's ongoing environment which directly or indirectly influence his behavior are described. Usually, the social history per se is obtained by the case worker. At times, these social data may be obtained by the psychologist, physician, or a vocational rehabilitation worker. Social histories may comprise a separate report; and, a statement or paragraph in the psychological report is considered to be a social history *statement*. These materials are usually quite important in the over-all evaluation of one's client.

Interview data form the second type of report, if used singularly. These findings are derived from a one-to-one conversation with the client (at times a group conference may be held) and include notes from individual therapy sessions, screening interviews, admission interviews, or pretest and posttest interviews. Several contacts with a client may be summarized in one report. Information obtained here is that of a first-hand nature, which is many times secured by the person preparing the report. This one-to-one, client-therapist information is very beneficial for use in reports as it gives the clinician a good indication of the patient's response to his environment.

In a *screening* evaluation many of the same principles apply as in the interview. The difference is that in the screening evaluation the primary objective is to obtain as much information as possible in a very brief form. This type of evaluation may only be of ten to twenty minutes duration. Brief tests may be given. This evaluation method is useful where large numbers of individuals must be seen in a limited time. Also, this type of session can be used very effectively to decide which patients need further, more detailed evaluations. A consulting psychiatrist, physician, psychologist, counselor, or social worker can use this method of patient appraisal quite readily.

Desirable in the *intellectual* evaluation is the administration of one or more standardized tests of intelligence. The tests may be of an individual or group nature. On occasion, with an uncooperative client, one must *infer* intellectual ability from his over-all behavioral and intellectual responses on an interview. This form of evaluation, with or without tests, may appear as a single report or as a portion of a more comprehensive write-up.

Whenever a client is involved in group or one-to-one psychotherapy it is the usual procedure to make a record of his progress. An informal type of reporting is through the use of *progress notes*, made on a session by session basis. Here, several therapy sessions may be written up as one progress note. A more elaborate report is called the *treatment summary*. This summary will usually appear as a separate report rather than inclusion in a psychological report per se. When the client has participated in a given number of therapy sessions, or for a given period of time, it is desirable to report on his longitudinal progress. Thus, a session by session account of his therapeutic interactions is written. The treatment summary may be very similar to any other psychological report, while the progress note is usually an informal paragraph or so on the patient's interim progress.

In the *comprehensive* psychological report one finds all of the pertinent data accumulated on the patient, current to the time the report is being written. It can very well include psychometric results, social and emotional observations, results from case conferences, interpretations, summaries, diagnoses, prognoses, recommendations, and precautions. Included in the psychometric results would be all tests administered including measures of intelligence, organicity, aptitude, achievement, interest, personality, and so forth. Certain items from the client's social history as well as from previous psychological reports may be included.

More will be discussed on each of the aforementioned types of reports later. Their inclusion at this point is intended only to present background material to aid the reader in the chapters to follow.

REPORT CONTENT

Certain identifying (or heading) information which includes the patient's name, age, sex, marital status, occupation, religious affiliation, the date or dates of the information procurement, the name of the clinician, the place the patient was seen, and the date of the report is basic to any report. In all reports (except the *social history statement* and the *treatment summary* where test results are usually not reported) the full names of the tests administered to the client are listed. If an interview was conducted, the word "Interview" is included in the category used to include the tests.

In the body of the report the very first narrative statement is usually the mention of the *purpose* of the psychological evaluation, interview, et cetera. This is more appropriately a one-sentence statement such as, "The client was referred to ___________ hospital (or clinic) on ___________, 19___, for a psychological evaluation; the school counselor, Mr. ___________, made the referral." Or, a statement such as, "Mr. ___________ was seen on ___________, 19___, for the purpose of a routine screening evaluation."

Following a statement of the purpose of the evaluation, usually comes a short description of the client's *physical appearance* and his *emotional response* to the testing or interview situation. Again, this is usually a very brief statement designed to communicate to the reader the examiner's impression of the client's overt physical appearance, behavior, and emotional tone at the time of the evaluation. This will be discussed in detail later.

The aforementioned considerations of a) identifying information, b) purpose of the evaluation, c) the client's physical appearance, and d) his initial emotional responses are basic and necessary to *any* type of report. These aspects form an important part of the report on which to build the evaluation and subsequent comments. Without proper identification, the future use of such an incomplete report is obvious. Likewise, a statement of the purpose of the report is necessary, since the usual procedure is to have some *reason* for doing an evaluation. The evaluation should not be made by a clinician for lack of something better to do. Even the screening evaluation is used to identify the client's handicaps, abilities, and emotionality in one area or another.

Then, with awareness of the just mentioned four categories of information, one proceeds to relate the *results* of the evaluation. In the case of the *interview* and the *treatment summary*, one obviously becomes cognizant of the need for the recording of accurate and sufficiently detailed, written notes. At times, it is quite difficult to recall the details of a given interview or of a certain treatment session from memory, especially if one has had several clients during a given day or week. There is hardly any substitute for pencil-and-paper notes, unless it is a mechanical tape recording.

After the clinician has made notes on all of the known facts concerning a given client, he has one of two courses of action to take in writing the remaining body of his report. First, he may list the facts and then make interpretive statements. Or secondly, he may integrate interpretive statements with facts throughout the course of the report. The procedures for both approaches will be discussed for each of the types of reports presented in later chapters.

The use of a *summary* and/or a *concluding statement* at the end of one's data presentation is optional. In certain cases it may be helpful to give a summary, but the preferences of the clinician and the nature of any given report will be the best guide for the writer.

As an aid to the reader of any report, either primary or secondary, some form of a *diagnosis* should be given. In an intellectual evaluation, only an intelligence quotient, mental age, or percentile may be given along with an intellectual classification such as "average," "borderline defective," and the like. An intellectual evaluation per se would not necessarily include a personality diagnosis; however, a supportive personality diagnosis (or "impression") could be given, providing there was sufficient reason for doing so. Any diagnosis must be based on the *facts presented in the report*, not something "pulled out of one's hat." In addition, the diagnosis should be compatible with the American Psychiatric Association's schedule of diagnostic categories, of course, this is not imperative; but, it does tend to promote standardization of diagnostic descriptions.

A *prognosis* should also accompany the report findings. Typically, the prognosis follows the diagnosis, since the diagnosis is the criterion *for* the prognosis. Put another way, the prognosis is the clinician's estimate or "educated guess" as to what the future holds for the client, as based on current findings.

Next, one usually lists any *recommendations* to be carried out on the basis of the report findings. These recommendations might be suggestions for further testing, psychological or medical, for psychotherapy, for employment placement or training, for continued psychiatric treatment, for the placement in special educational classes, or for termination of treatment and therapy. The actual list of possible recommendations is almost astronomical as any recommendations are highly contingent upon the circumstances and intellectual-emotional-physical realm of the patient's specific situation. Again, like the diagnosis, the recommendations should be based only upon the findings presented in the report itself and not merely pulled out of thin air.

Finally, in the event that the client is presently or potentially dangerous to himself or to others, then a statement should be made to this effect under the heading, "precautions." For example, a simple statement such as "suicidal" may suffice; on the other hand, a detailed statement or paragraph might be necessary to explain the circumstances which circumscribe a statement of precaution.

This chapter is intended to provide the reader with a brief sketch of the global nature of the psychological report. With these principles in mind it is hoped that the reader will have a more operational framework within which to view the report. Chapter III will briefly describe some aspects of organization for psychological reports.

ORGANIZATION OF THE REPORT

As mentioned earlier, no attempt will be made to instruct the reader in the proper usage of English grammar. Several good publications are currently on the market for that purpose. Be that as it may, there are certain points that should be considered in the composition of psychological reports.

First of all, and most essential, one should organize or group similar information in the report. The reader's job will be made easier. For example, when speaking of organic findings, do not superimpose personality data unless it has a *direct* bearing on organicity. In other words, keep such information as physical appearance of the client, his emotional response to the testing or interview situation, the test findings, and so on, separate. Later in the report, perhaps in the summary, the findings of several areas can be combined. At times it may be difficult for one to separate one evaluatory area from another, especially if there are overlapping findings.

Secondly, and similarly important, write complete sentences, avoid misspelled words, and obvious grammatical errors. Other than a grammatically correct report being easier to read, it is also a reflection of the writer's writing skill, as well as educational, intellectual, and professional competence. True, if the clinician has a secretary who is proficient in the realm of grammar and composition, then he can perhaps dodge his own shortcomings. However, one may not be so lucky—you may have to proofread and correct your own report.

A third point to bear in mind is that it is most important to differentiate between *facts obtained* and *clinical interpretations* of these facts. This is especially important when presenting results on projective and subjective tests, where the *facts* may be difficult to separate from the clinician's own inferences of these data. In the reporting of test results, if the client seemed to have inadvertently "invalidated" the test through his being distracted by some extraneous event, the clinician would state his opinion as to the reliability of the test scores made by the client.

The fourth point is that the writer should clearly distinguish between a patient's comment and a clinical interpretation of that comment. It may seem facetious to some to say that this is best done through the use of quotation marks. However, some writers unwittingly commit this error. If you are recording a client's verbatim comment for purposes of illustration in the report— fine—but, use quotation marks. When quoting a lengthy patient discourse the writer may have to use elipses (three periods as . . .) thereby only presenting the most pertinent statements made by the client. Examples will be given later. Note that one uses *elipses* (. . .) for indicating *omissions* in quoted material, while the dash (-- or —) is used to indicate a *pause* in the verbalization. The proper and consistent use of these symbols will insure better organization and style in your reports.

Fifth, one may feel free to write up a psychological report in the *past, present,* and *future* tense, or any one of the three (except exclusively in the future tense). One school of thought is that the testing, interview, and social history data represents a past undertaking at the time you begin writing the report. There is a certain amount of validity in this assumption: what has happened, has happened. Conversely, the psychological report can be viewed as a write-up containing an evaluation of the client's *present status* and level of specific and general functioning. From this view one would write the report in the present tense. No one would wisely write a report entirely in the future tense, unless the clinician is a mystic. Probably more appropriately the report would be written in the past, present, *and* future.

The test results, parts of the social history, and certain aspects of the interview data would involve a past event. Interpretations, evaluations, summaries of the data, and the diagnosis of the client would fit well into the present tense. Then, the prognosis, recommendations, and precautions would seem to imply future statuses or events. While the familiar "research paper" is usually written in the past tense, the psychological evaluation more appropriately is an analysis of ongoing processes in the client's behavioral repertoire. One's practical definition of the past, present, and future will obviously determine when to use these time-space continuums.

Common practice in report writing is to construct it in a start to finish or *chronological* order of presentation. Beginning with identification of the patient, one next lists the tests and interviews conducted. The purpose of the evaluation follows as a brief statement, usually designating the persons or group making the referral. Next comes a short description of the client's physical appearance and physical history data. Comments on the client's response to the evaluation session would probably follow.

The body of the report, for example, can include many items, depending on whether or not it is an interview, intellectual evaluation, or a complete psychological evaluation. These content areas will be discussed separately in Chapters VII through XII.

The summary and conclusion sections of a report are optional and depend on the over-all nature of the report and the needs of the writer and proposed readers. If you use a summary section in your report, this is the crux of your presentation. It gives the reader a brief, over-all sketch of the client's functioning. Resultantly, it should summarize all facts in a brief manner, without introducing new data. Probably it would be limited to a few sentences or a short paragraph at the most. The summary in a psychological report is somewhat analogous to an "abstract" of an article in a professional journal. The conclusions of a report (if used) will include the highlights of the summary and therefore lead directly to a diagnosis. New material is neither introduced in the summary nor in the conclusion. In the case of conflicting evidence or findings, the conclusion might be used to encompass ideas which justify a multiple diagnosis; or, to present rationale for making a differential diagnosis. More will be discussed on diagnostic methods in Chapter VI.

To aid the report writer in making an outline, the following sample, comprehensive outline is presented. It should be noted that not all of the areas in this outline would be used in any one report.

I. IDENTIFYING DATA
   A. Client's name, age, sex, marital status.
   B. Date of evaluation.
   C. Place of evaluation.
   D. Date of report.
   E. Clinician's name and credentials (cf.: heading XVI).

II. TESTS ADMINISTERED
   A. Interviews.
   B. Intellectual measures (specify).
   C. Organic measures (specify).
   D. Personality measures (specify).
   E. Aptitude or achievement measures (specify).
   F. Interest measures (specify).
   G. Special tests (specify).

III. PURPOSE OF EVALUATION
   A. Purpose (routine or special).
   B. Person or group making the referral.
   C. Name of facility making the referral.

IV. PHYSICAL APPEARANCE AND EMOTIONALITY
   A. Client's general state of health (present and past).
   B. Client's grooming and dress.
   C. Client's emotional response to the evaluation session.
   D. Client's performance response to the evaluation.

V. SOCIAL HISTORY STATEMENT
   A. Home, family, and living conditions of the client.
   B. Employment history, job skills, and finances.
   C. Marriage and family adjustment.
   D. Methods of adjusting to stress.
   E. Education.
   F. Previous psychiatric treatment.
   G. Religious activities.

VI. INTELLECTUAL FINDINGS
   A. Results of intelligence, aptitude, and achievement tests.
   B. Intellectual alertness.
   C. Strengths and weaknesses in various intellectual realms.
   D. Task approach.
   E. Et cetera.

VII. ORGANIC FINDINGS
   A. Psychomotor coordination (obvious behavior).
   B. Test results.
   C. Et cetera.

VIII. PERSONALITY FINDINGS
  A. Obvious personality response during testing.
  B. Interview data.
  C. Test results.
  D. Et cetera.

IX. INTEREST AND VOCATIONAL FINDINGS
  A. Interview data.
  B. Test results.
  C. Et cetera.

X. SUMMARY (optional)
  A. High points of all data presented.
  B. No new data introduced.

XI. CONCLUSIONS (optional)
  A. High points of summary.
  B. Basis for multiple diagnosis.
  C. Basis for differential diagnosis.

XII. DIAGNOSIS
  A. The types of diagnosis.
    1. *Impression* diagnosis.
    2. *Tentative* diagnosis.
    3. *Final* (absolute) diagnosis.
    4. *Multiple* diagnosis.
  B. The diagnosis is based on all data in the report.
  C. There may be a *primary* and a *secondary* diagnosis, in this sequence.
  D. Use American Psychiatric Association diagnostic classification system.
  E. Use a behavioral classification system.

XIII. PROGNOSIS
  A. Based on the diagnosis.
  B. There can be a prognosis for the
    1. present episode,
    2. future adjustment.

XIV. PRECAUTIONS (when justified)
  A. To alert the reader to potential harm the client might be to himself or others.
  B. Examples are "suicidal," "homicidal," "security risk," and "elopement."

XV.   RECOMMENDATIONS
- A.   Based on over-all findings, including the diagnosis, prognosis, and precautions.
- B.   Examples are the following.
    1. Further specialized testing.
    2. Neurological examination.
    3. Psychotherapy, individual or group.
    4. Placement in special classes or training areas.
    5. Vocational rehabilitation.
    6. Institutionalization.
    7. Medical examination.
    8. Discontinuance of specific therapy.
    9. Discontinuance of hospitalization.
    10. Et cetera.

XVI.   SIGNATURE BLOCK
- A.   Clinician's name.
- B.   Clinician's credentials.
- C.   Clinician's signature.

In the foregoing sixteen outlined areas, not all will normally be used in any one evaluation. Certain types of reports, such as a comprehensive psychological, may require all areas. Also, certain of these areas are more common to a counseling setting and others to a clinical setting. Nevertheless, they are listed so as to give an over-all range of possible report content areas.

In any event, areas I, II, III, XII, XIII, XV, and XVI will be used for every type of report. The inclusion of other areas is dependent upon the type of evaluation which was conducted, the future use of the report, and the examiner's preferences. Still, the classification sequence of data (from I to XVI) is the recommended chronological format to follow.

Using another example, if the report is based on interview data alone, then all of the previously mentioned "psychometric" areas of the report will be omitted, i.e. the test categories. However, one can very well *infer* intellectual, personality, interest, and other data from an interview alone, and the report categories might be used here. But, one would certainly clarify in the report that these were *impressions* or *inferences* and not test findings per se.

One other point of significance is that even though the report *outline* has various headings, these headings are not necessarily used in a report. It is acceptable to report findings without physical headings on the actual typed report. The writer's personal preferences, and those of his reading audience will dictate whether or not he uses headings preceding a given data area.

A sample outline of a typical report is presented next.

    I.   Identifying data.
   II.   Tests administered.
  III.   Purpose of the evaluation.
  IV.   Intellectual and organic findings.
   V.   Personality findings.
  VI.   Diagnosis.
 VII.   Prognosis.
VIII.   Recommendations.
  IX.   Signature block.

Note that the aforementioned short outline did not use separate categories for intellectual and organic findings (this is frequently done unless several tests of organicity have been administered). Also, a summary and conclusion section was not included. This is only one of many types of possible outlines in actual practice. Here, one may very well write-in these headings on the actual report. Another type of report outline, even more simple, is the following.

    I.   Identifying data.
   II.   Tests administered.
  III.   Results of the evaluation.
  IV.   Diagnosis.
   V.   Recommendations.
  VI.   Signature block.

This six-point outline is probably the shortest form which one should use. Any attempt to be more concise would probably necessitate the omission of important material. At the very least, a much shortened form would force one to group many types of information thereby creating a cluttered report.

Regardless of whether or not official, written headings are actually put on the physical report, the data presented should follow an outline. This is just good organizational procedure. With an outline in mind, one is able to write a chronological, logical, coherent, and easily read report. It would be very confusing to the reader if the report writer were in one sentence talking about intellectual ability and in the next, discussing emotional factors without appropriate transitional sentences or paragraphs. The reader should not have to search throughout the report to find similar information. Where applicable, one should group test results in terms of poor, fair, average, or superior performance (or any other equivalent grouping). For example, "the client performed *average* on subtests *a*, *b*, and *c*; but, he displayed *poor* ability on subtests *d*, *e*, and *f*." The report writer will have to group test results on the basis of the client's scores and the types of tests being used. The ways of describing and grouping information are virtually endless.

After one has written several reports a personal style will come easier, and the organization of the material will be simplified. It is wise to keep in mind that certain things must be communicated; and when these have been done the reader will benefit more from the report. Several other points should be considered when writing any report. First, one must have something to communicate; second, the communication should follow some logical order of presentation; third, it should be written with coherence; fourth, the report should not contain misspelled words; fifth, the report should not engulf the reader in language he cannot understand; sixth, the report findings should lead to a diagnosis and a prognosis; and finally, the report should present results on which to base one's recommendations. All reports should be signed.

The report writer should ask himself the following questions *before* writing any report:

1. Do I have the interview and test data readily available to use?
2. Are my test data scored and interpreted with accuracy?
3. Do I have a plan for the report?
4. Have I prepared an outline (written or mental) to follow in writing the report?
5. Who will my readers be?
6. How can I write a report that will be functional to the readers?
7. What findings are to be included in the report?
8. How can I present and interpret these findings most effectively?
9. Can all ambiguous terms be defined and clarified?
10. Am I prepared to let the results lead to a conclusion, rather than trying to find results to support my preconceived biases about the client?

After a rough draft of the report has been written, prior to having it typed, the writer should then ask himself these questions:

1. Is my outline or mechanical style appropriate to the type of report being written?
2. Have I included all relevant data in this report?
3. Is the information organized in an effective manner?
4. Is the writing clear, coherent, logical, and easy to read?
5. Have I corrected all obvious grammatical errors?
6. Are there any misspelled words or ambiguous, undefined terms?
7. Is my summary concise and relevant?
8. Do the results lead to a diagnosis? To a prognosis?
9. Are my recommendations sound, wise, and feasible? Are they specific and operational?
10. Have I read the report in its entirety at least once after writing?

Finally, after the preceding twenty questions have been considered on any report, the following suggestions are given for the report writer.

First, after making the rough draft of the report, make all necessary corrections.

Second, reread the draft with the corrections, and make any additional corrections needed.

Third, lay the report aside for a few hours (if you have the time) then read the corrected report again to see if it still sounds like a good report.

Fourth, if the report passes your final inspection, give it to your typist for typing—request at least one copy for your records.

Only when all of the so-called "facts" are available is the psychologist (or other professional) able to write an intelligent report. Too well do we know that one's own intellectual level or academic credentials do not in themselves guarantee a good, clear, understandable, and comprehensive report. A little intellectual "elbow grease" goes a long way toward creating an adequate piece of writing. The psychological report is no exception. With practice comes skill and ease in writing.

For the psychological report to be correct, tests should be administered with skill and interpreted correctly. Other data should indicate the dynamics which ultimately and logically lead to a diagnosis, indicate a prognosis, and give the writer foundations on which to base his personal recommendations for the client's rehabilitation.

Chapter IV

LANGUAGE OF THE REPORT

As DISCUSSED in previous chapters, communication is the goal of the psychological report. Without communication of ideas, intellectual interaction does not occur. Two forms of communication, spoken and written, are basic to man's socialization. The report, in essence, is a concise, to-the-point communication of facts and interpretations through the expression of symbolic thought—written language.

For effective communication one must write reports in a manner which the potential reader can easily understand. There is no place for clinician-coined phraseology and psychological double-talk. One is not aiming for a media such as "Newspeak" as did Orwell in his book, *1984.* One should attempt to interact in a clear manner with the reader. Albert Einstein once remarked:

> Although words exist for the most part for the transmission of ideas, there are some which produce such violent disturbances in our feelings that the role they play in the transmission of ideas is lost in the background.

This should be food for thought. The improper use of words and phraseology can very well cloud the communication to such an extent that one cannot "see the forest for the trees." It may be difficult at times to write in an effective manner—and none of us are beyond flaw—but, one should make a zealous attempt to do so. A French poet of the Romantic Period, Lamartine, said in 1832, "The finest lines are those we cannot write." When writing the psychological report (or at least the first one) one may very well feel as Lamartine did. With effort, however, one can quite readily learn to communicate in an effective manner.

Language used in the psychological report is quite similar to that used in any other type of report, paper, or article. The difference, though small, is that one should make every effort to communicate his ideas in an *extremely* clear and coherent manner. It is really not difficult. Why? Because in the report one states facts, makes interpretations, and derives conclusions from these facts and interpretations. The procedure is comparable to any situation where one attempts to systematically arrive at conclusions from an assorted group of data; it is the common process of deductive reasoning. The clinician should write reports in a language style in which he is most comfortable. That is, do not consciously attempt to use a vocabulary or sentence style beyond your comfortable writing range. Do not attempt to impress your reader with a grandiose vocabulary which he may or may not clearly understand. It is much better to communicate in an effective manner, using simple words, than it is to become entangled in a grammatical salad which tends to confuse the reader.

The "coining" of psychological terms, without supportive definitions is definitely taboo in the report. If, for example, a quotation from the client includes coined terms, word-salad, and the like, then this should be appropriately distinguished from the comments of the therapist. Similarly, words or phrases common to a given psychologist or his theory which may be misinterpreted by the reader should also be fully explained. It is well to bear in mind that the problem of communication also exists *among* psychologists and other practitioners. It is much better to say that a patient has a pathological attachment of a dependent nature toward his mother than to say that he has an "Oedipus Complex." As professionals tend to disagree on diagnoses many times, the communication of *descriptive* behavior is much better than psychological condensation with subsequent labels. You should describe the patient's behavior so completely so as to enable the reader to arrive at a diagnosis on the descriptions you give. After all, clinicians do tend to differ in their rationale for arriving at certain diagnoses.

To restate a point made earlier, if it is necessary or desirable to use verbatim material from a test protocol or from an interview with the client, be sure to *differentiate* the client's statements from yours by using quotation marks. And, when using verbatim material obtained from a client, *keep it verbatim!* Do not change his sentence structure, or phraseology just because it "doesn't sound sophisticated." The exact wording which the client uses has important diagnostic implications and alerts the professional to the client's ideation.

The next point of importance in regard to report language is in the use of *specialized terms or concepts.* By this is meant that inherent in the educational background of a given clinician one finds certain therapeutic orientations. For example, there are concepts and words common to the Freudians, the Rogerians, and the Jungians. This is fine. However, the reader of the report may not have a working vocabulary of all unique terms used by the many psychological theorists. As a result, such terms as Freud's "Superego" may not have universal-specific meaning to a follower of another frame of reference. Similarly, such terms as Oedipus Complex, ego-alien, erg, press, drive-strength, emotional homeostasis, and the like are terms specific to certain theories and their founders. Rather than use such terms in a report it is much better to be more specific and describe behavior in terms of common, everyday language. By using "common English" one can close many communication gaps and thereby prevent numerous misinterpretations of patient data. A quite common psychological term, "self-actualization," is a good example of ambiguity. To some it means a level of self-achievement and fulfillment, attained by only a few, well-adjusted individuals who are approaching a psychological utopia. To others, the term means the fullest realization of one's potentials, relative to one's inherent capacity. To further confuse the definition of self-actualization, one could feasibly be self-actualized in a positive as well as a negative way—one could realize his fullest potential as a criminal or as a philanthropist! Hence, communication is more effective in a report when one *describes behavior symptomatically and concretely* rather than through the use of theoretical-specific terms.

Another important point to consider is in the use of certain quantitative terms such as "below average," "average," "above average," "dull-normal," "excellent," and so forth. Fortunately, most terms of this type have an *average* amount of universal meaning to most clinicians. But, when in doubt, it is wise to clarify categories such as these. For example, the term "dull-normal" corresponds to an Intelligence Quotient between 80 and 89 by Wechsler standards; however, there are other definitions. Similarly, when using the term "average" one must clarify whether or not the client is average in a certain skill in relation to the population as a whole, to a specific sub-group, or in relation to his *own* over-all performance. Obviously, these are minor details but they may make a difference in the reader's interpretations of certain types of information.

It is essential that you *mean what you write.* Do not commit the error of being vague or ambiguous thereby writing with the hope that the reader will "read between the lines" and fill in communication gaps for you. Be as brief as possible in your communication but do not omit important details merely for the sake of brevity. Going further, watch your sentence structure. As you know, the simple injection of a comma in a certain place in the sentence can drastically change the meaning of the entire sentence. To exemplify, consider the following two sentences, "The client displayed dull, normal intelligence"; or, "The client displayed dull normal intelligence." The first apparently says that the patient is psychologically dull, but has normal intelligence. In the second sentence it was implied that the patient's intellectual functioning was in the *dull normal* area. Two completely different ideas were presented.

One is treading on thin ice when he writes things that cannot be supported. Strangely enough, this is a common occurrence in psychological reports. Too often the writer will say such things as "the client *has* average intelligence"; "he *is* hostile"; "he *is* suspicious"; et cetera. As a clinician (and human being) one *does not know* if the client *has* average intelligence, if he *is* hostile, or if he *is* suspicious. What one really means is that the client *performed* in an average manner on a given intelligence test, or that he *displayed* suspicious or hostile behavior through his verbal comments or overt actions. You can never be absolute about these things since you *do not really know for sure*! You can only deduct and interpret and speculate. To take another situation, you may say that a patient *has* a visual disturbance simply because he tells you that he cannot see the questions in the test booklet; however, he may be misleading you! He might very well be a negativistic or a depressed person who readily makes sundry excuses to avoid exerting himself.

Consider another case in psychological wording. When you write, "the patient exhibited paranoid behavior, and is therefore clearly schizophrenic," one leaves out many behavior specifics. Obviously, this statement has several gross errors. First, it is stated that the patient *has* paranoid behavior (an absolute) but the reader has no indication as to the *type*. Is this patient suspicious, evasive, guarded in his responses, exhibiting delusions of persecution or grandeur; is he overtly or covertly appearing hostile; or, is this so-called behavior actual or implied? The phrase, "paranoid behavior" tells the reader nothing specific. Secondly, in the sentence there is a logical inference that *because* this patient exhibited paranoid behavior, *then* he *must* be schizophrenic! Is it not possible that this patient could be psychoneurotic with a few transient thoughts, feelings, or ideas which were paranoid *in character*? Thirdly, a sin of absolutism has been committed. The statement, "is therefore clearly schizophrenic," leaves little room for error on the part of the clinician.

For a comparison of the ambiguous statement just presented the following symptomatic (and somewhat more communicative) statement is given, "The patient displayed attitudes which *seemed* to be persecutory and suspicious in nature as *his comments* were very accusing toward people, since *he said* the people were 'no good' and that they were trying to poison him. These feelings of the patient *appear* to be paranoid in character and are therefore *indicative* of schizophrenic thinking." Without any doubt it takes longer to describe *symptoms* of behavior than it does to merely make an absolute summary statement. By describing behavior symptomatically one provides a great deal more information for the reader.

Another comment on absolutism in writing should be made. The use of words such as "seems," "appears," "apparently," "probably," "possibly," and others gives the writer as much absolutism as he needs. Remember, when testing a client you are only measuring *responses* to a test stimulus; and, when interviewing you are only recording *responses* to your interview statements. There is no way to *completely know* how a person *really* feels and thinks—one merely makes observations and inferences from the information received.

Going further, it is extremely important that the writer avoids the use of *abbreviations* unless they are spelled out at least once in the report. The reason should be apparent. Since any number of abbreviations could possibly mean the same thing this would only further confuse the reader. Common errors are to make use of such abbreviations as one would derive from the name of a test, such as WAIS, TAT, QT, MMPI, MFD, BVMG, and CPI. You may know some of these; others may be totally new to you. The implications are obvious, or should be. Similarly, it is not good writing to use such short-cuts as IQ, MQ, SQ, or FSIQ. The point is that if you use any term in your report which has a convenient abbreviation, do not use it as an end in itself. Spell out at least once all terms used in the report, preferably when they are first mentioned. A final note here is that when describing performance on any test, do not abbreviate the subtest names; spell out these names.

Words should be used properly in any report. By this is meant that one should be aware of the correct definitions of all words used. Remember that the reader may be interpreting the word differently than did the writer. On the other hand, it is virtually impossible for any writer to be certain that the words he chose will be "correctly" interpreted by the reader. This is true of any written material. However, through the writer's avoidance of controversial and inherently ambiguous terms many of the possible errors in communication can be avoided. If ambiguous terms must be used to present a point, be sure that this ambiguity is qualified or defined.

Another common error in psychological report writing is to clutter the report with negative statements of things that *did not* happen. For example, one occasionally finds statements like, "The client had no apparent physical ailments and did not wear glasses." Through the use of the *positive*, one could better write this sentence by saying that "The client appeared in good physical health." It is also rather useless to say that "The patient has no organic pathology inasmuch as his neurological examination and his performance on the *Bender Visual Motor Gestalt* test were normal." Why not say, "Neurological examination and results from the psychometric examination were well within normal limits?" The case against negative statements is that if it did not happen, why bother to mention it? Almost all report information can be stated in the positive.

There are some instances when a combination of positive and negative statements must be made. For instance, one might find it necessary to say, "The patient showed minimal organic signs on the *Bender Visual Motor Gestalt* test; but, a follow-up neurological examination and electroencephalogram ruled out any possibility of intracranial pathology." Here, one uses a negative clause to qualify a preceding clause. In the final analysis, the writer will have to decide for himself just how he should phrase his sentences to achieve the most desirable report for his readers.

Chapter V

GUIDANCE COUNSELORS, CLINICAL PSYCHOLOGISTS, AND REPORTS

THE PRINCIPLES of psychological report writing remain the same, regardless of who writes one. However, there are some points which seem to be specific to certain professional settings. Reports written by public or private school guidance counselors may differ somewhat from those prepared by clinical psychologists. The terms, "guidance counselors" and "clinical psychologists," are used in this chapter to distinguish between those clinicians who operate within different organizational frameworks. Functionally, the guidance counselor can very well be a clinical psychologist, and vice versa.

The clinical psychologist is referred to here as any individual who a) has had clinical training, irrespective of his professional duties; b) who may be employed in a private or public out-patient clinic; or c) who may be employed in a private or public in-patient psychiatric institution. Usually, the clinical psychologist will deal with the more severe cases of emotional and intellectual disorders in a psychiatric center; however, he may be working in a) the public school counseling role; b) a public or private school psychological services center; or c) as a teacher in a college or university. The lines are at times not easily drawn, due to an overlapping of professional roles. For simplification it is assumed that the clinical psychologist more *commonly* works in the psychiatric setting whereas the counselor more *commonly* is employed in the educational environment.

GUIDANCE COUNSELORS AND REPORTS

The counselor in the public or private school setting has duties rather unique to his profession. In particular, there is an emphasis upon counseling students with minor (usually nonpsychotic) adjustment problems. Additionally, such duties as student orientation, personnel services, student placement, group testing, and others are somewhat routine. The counselor will prepare brief "notes" on student and parent-pupil conferences, as well as write several types of psychological reports.

In the counseling role one may prepare any one of several types of reports. Each of these reports will serve an individual purpose in the realm of counseling. These reports can come under one or more of the following six categories (as well as others):

1. Counseling interview summary.
2. Psychological evaluations.
3. Cumulative record notes.
4. Referral reports.
5. Reports to teachers.
6. Reports to parents.

These six report areas are not meant to be limiting in terms of the possible types of reports a counselor may prepare. Yet, they do represent some major reporting areas.

Counseling Interview Summary

This report is used to record interview notes obtained from one-to-one or group counseling sessions of any type. It serves as a chronological record of interview data supplied by the client, observations of the client's overt behavior, and any of the counselor's interpretations. Additionally, the report may be facilitated by a typed transcription from a mechanical tape recording of a therapy session. The interview summary is a very important part of report writing because it provides a record of therapy contacts as well as material on which to plan future counseling sessions. Depending on school policy, the report may or may not be filed in the student's cumulative record folder; however, the counselor will always maintain a copy himself.

Psychological Evaluation

The psychological evaluation, whether prepared by a counselor or clinical psychologist, is essentially the same. Thus, the guidelines for one clinician apply to another. This evaluation report may well include a) reasons for the student's referral to the counselor; b) specific purpose of the evaluation; c) observations of the student's behavior; and d) interview and psychometric results. It may be that the counselor has a need to prepare two separate reports as a result of a given student's evaluation. The first might be a report to the teacher or principal; and, the second may be for the counselor's files or for an outside treatment center. The rules for primary and secondary readers which were discussed in Chapter II may well apply here.

A report to the teacher may characteristically be written in symptomatic terms as well as having recommendations for the teacher's follow-up. The report for the school's files or to a referral agency will similarly be written in symptomatic terms but will more than likely contain certain technical language of test findings, a clinical diagnosis, and recommendations. It goes without saying that any report that might find its way into the hands of lay persons should not contain a clinical diagnosis—a diagnostic summary in lay terms would be more appropriate.

Cumulative Record Notes

These notes are not regarded as psychological reports as such. They are more thought of in terms of being brief comments (many times written in longhand) on student observations, achievement or aptitude test results, or placement interviews. A separate report is usually not written, as these comments are usually recorded direct in the student's cumulative record or counseling folder. Nevertheless, they are significant reporting procedures.

Referral Reports

The referral report may occur as the result of a teacher or principal's request for a student evaluation. On the other hand, this type of report can be thought of in terms of a communication to a referral agency such as a school psychological clinic, an out-patient psychiatric clinic, or a state psychiatric hospital or training facility. When preparing a report for an extra-school agency, one usually writes as complete a report as possible which includes all relevant data obtained on the student. A psychological evaluation report format may be used here quite well.

The referral report can also be considered as a *comprehensive psychological examination*, if it is a multifunction examination. When sending out a report of this type, it may be necessary to send copies of test answer sheets or test profile sheets to the agency. In any event, on a report such as this one must consider the legal realms—it may be necessary to obtain a medical release.

Reports to Teachers

Official reports to teachers are not nearly as common as other types of reports. But, there may be a special circumstance (such as a report going to a teacher in a special education center) where a teacher's report may be desirable. A report going to a regular or special teacher should include only that information that the teacher can use. The teacher's report should be more general in scope than a "clinical report" would be—it should concentrate on reporting the student's level of functioning in operational terms. Any report to a teacher should include several recommendations which can apply to the classroom situation, thereby aiding the work of the teacher.

Reports to Parents

A written report to a parent *should not be made* except in a very few rare cases. It is too easy for a parent to misinterpret any and all of the report data. A few parents with professional or similar status may view a counselor's report objectively; but, even they may interpret the report in a distorted manner. If a parent demands a report (very few will) then the counselor can prepare a very generalized one. In no instance should a report to a parent include such terms as "IQ" or "schizophrenic."

The counselor is usually on safe ground if he reports intellectual data in terms of "average," "above average," or "below average" and personality data in terms of "socially withdrawn," "adequate social skills for his age," and the like. *Never use clinical terminology or clinical diagnoses in any report going to a parent!* If the student is found to be mentally retarded, gifted, or severely emotionally disturbed, it is much better to call the parents in for a conference than to disclose these findings through an "official" report. The same is true for any other types of reports.

There is no adequate substitute for the counselor's personal interpretation of the findings to the parent. One last word, *if* an official report to a parent *must* be made, write the report with the educational level of the parent in mind.

The counselor in the school setting may have fewer reports to write than the clinical psychologist. The counselor will many times make informal "notes" in his counseling records or in the student's cumulative record folder whereas an officially typed report may not be necessary. It should be stressed, however, that any counselor-student contact should be recorded in some manner so as to provide a chronological record of the student's over-all progress. To repeat, the counselor will more frequently write comprehensive psychological reports on referral cases (incoming and referrals out) than in any other situation. This includes referrals from a teacher to the counselor as well as referrals from the counselor to an outside person or agency. In any instance where a report must be sent on a student to an outside agency (not under the school's auspices), a legal release form of confidential information must be processed. This release form may be initiated by either the requesting agency or by the counselor. Several sample forms are illustrated later in Chapter XIV.

CLINICAL PSYCHOLOGISTS AND REPORTS

The clinical psychologist will undoubtedly have more different *types* of reports to write than will the counselor. Reports made by the psychologist in a clinical setting will usually be filed in the patient's medical record folder. Therefore, any number of professional persons employed by a given treatment facility will have access to these records. It is for interdisciplinary reasons that clarity of one's terminology and communication are essential. The types of reports used in the clinical setting, in part, usually include:

1. Screening of incoming patients.
2. Staffing reports.
3. Complete psychological evaluations.
4. Evaluations for treatment programming.
5. Individual psychotherapy interview notes.
6. Group psychotherapy notes.

7. Progress notes.
8. Evaluations in court cases.
9. Evaluations for continued hospitalization.
10. Evaluations for patient discharges.

To be sure, these ten types of reports do not include all of the possible types in use. However, most will come under these general categories. For patients involved in occupational, recreational, vocational, music, dance, and similar types of special therapy, the clinical psychologist is not usually the therapist in charge. These special forms of therapeutic intervention often are directed by the person in charge of the vocational rehabilitation services or the activity therapy sections of one's facility.

Screening of Incoming Patients

Different State laws, as well as local procedures, will usually determine the nature and extent of evaluations of incoming patients. In some cases, incoming patients must be seen by a psychologist or psychiatrist within twenty-four hours after admission; in other cases the patient must be seen within five days; in still other situations there may not be any time limit. In any event, all patients are usually seen at least once after admission for a diagnostic evaluation. This evaluation may consist of a short interview, or it may consist of an interview plus the administration of one or more psychological tests. Nevertheless, the screening session will result in a brief psychological report which usually includes a) a short history leading up to the patient's admission; b) a description of the present symptomology; c) a diagnosis; d) a prognosis; e) immediate treatment recommendations, including psychiatric and medical areas; and f) precautions, if any.

Staffing Reports

The staffing report can be considered to be almost synonymous with the incoming patient screening procedures. However, the staffing report may be conducted by several psychiatric team members. On the basis of this patient "staffing" a report will usually be written by the senior team member or psychologist. Similarly, the staffing report can very well be the result of a follow-up patient analysis; in this case the evaluation would not be considered a screening session, but a progress evaluation session.

Complete Psychological Evaluations

After a patient has been accepted for treatment in a psychiatric facility, it may be desirable to conduct a comprehensive psychological evaluation. This would be especially desirable whereby brain damage, mental retardation, or special emotional ramifications were suspected. Also, it is desirable to conduct a comprehensive psychological evaluation on *every* patient admitted to an in-patient facility. However, many institutions are under-staffed, and it is a physical impossibility for a handful of clinicians to give a thorough psychometric evaluation to each patient upon admission. Therefore, the initial screening or staffing evaluation often has to suffice for other types of immediate evaluations. On the other hand, in a private in-patient or out-patient clinic, it may be quite feasible to conduct a comprehensive evaluation on each incoming patient.

Evaluations for Treatment Programming

In many cases the initial screening, staffing, or comprehensive psychological work-up may take the place of a special evaluation for treatment programming. However, after several days or weeks of staff observations have been made, it may be desirable to conduct a special treatment evaluation. Here, a patient may be tested and interviewed for certain institutional work assignments, special treatment workshops, vocational rehabilitation, and the like. Or, it may appear that a given patient would respond more effectively to group than to individual psychotherapy and vice versa. This programming evaluation is considered here to be a follow-up procedure after the patient has been institutionalized (or functioning as an out-patient) for a period of time. This programming procedure may be the work of a single psychologist or the result of a team level decision.

Individual Psychotherapy Interview Notes

Reports should be routinely made on all individual psychotherapy sessions in either an in-patient or an out-patient setting.

These notes can be very valuable for use in planning future interviews as well as for use in ascertaining the patient's progress through the course of therapy. Since an individual therapy session may last from one-half to one full hour on the average, it is possible that as many as three to five pages would comprise a report—this would depend upon the types of information included in the report. Generally, notes on an individual psychotherapy session would consist of behavioral observations, selected points on the patient's thinking, and any significant statements made by the patient. For practical purposes, these notes would probably not be more than one-half to one full page written on each treatment session; at the least, there should be no less than one paragraph per session.

Group Psychotherapy Notes

As with individual therapy notes, one may write reports on a patient's sociopersonal interactions occurring in the group psychotherapy sessions. In the group setting the clinician may make notes on all patients who contribute something to the total discussion. The clinician may wish to maintain a master note file which describes the group session *in toto*; however, when reporting group therapy notes for placement in a given patient's file only those comments which apply to that particular patient will be recorded in his file. For example, if in a given group session there are six patients who take part in the discussion, then there will be six *separate* reports (or notes) which will be placed in each of these patient's respective files. Only the observations, interactions, and clinician's comments which apply to a given patient will be placed in his record folder. Obstensibly, then, the group therapy notes will be much shorter in length than one would expect to find as a result of an hour long one-to-one patient interview.

Progress Notes

The progress note may be synonymous with the individual or group psychotherapy notes, if the clinician's only contact with a given patient is in the therapy session. Another use for the progress note is in the recording of a short note (perhaps no more than one paragraph) which results from an informal patient contact. This informal contact might be one on the patient's wards.

Evaluations in Court Cases

From time to time a clinical psychologist may be asked by his employer or directly by the local or state courts to conduct a a complete, diagnostic evaluation on a given client. This client might be receiving out-patient or in-patient psychotherapy, as well as other forms of treatment. He may be receiving no therapy. The client may be awaiting a court hearing or trial while being incarcerated in a local jail, or other holding facility. Also, the client might be confined in a psychiatric facility on a temporary basis while criminal charges are pending in the courts. In any event, the psychological evaluation may be requested for the purposes of a) ascertaining legal sanity or insanity of the client; b) determining whether or not the client is sufficiently stable to stand trail in the courts; or c) establishing the possibility of the client being harmful to himself or to others.

In evaluations which may be admissible as court evidence there may be certain diagnostic tests which are required; these may or may not be defined by the court. Usually, one or two each of measures of personality, intelligence, and organicity will be required, along with a diagnostic interview session. Under few circumstances would less than two or three psychological tests be adequate for an evaluation to be submitted to the courts. There are times, however, when the testimony of (or a statement by) an "expert witness" may be used. A licensed psychiatrist or psychologist may act as this expert in a psychiatric competency hearing or trial. Finally, it goes without saying that any psychological report to be used in court proceedings should be carefully thought out and well written. This is true for all other reports as well.

Evaluations for Continued Hospitalization

Periodically, the clinician will be requested to evaluate a patient to see whether or not continued hospitalization is feasible and necessary. This evaluation will be required at certain intervals, subject to local and state policies and laws. In some cases, a patient must be reevaluated each thirty or sixty days; in others, the interval may be longer. The follow-up evaluative procedures may be different for a voluntary patient than for a patient committed by the court. Nonetheless, any patient should be reevaluated at periodic intervals whether or not it is required by law or local policy—the patient deserves this much. On an evaluation for continued hospitalization, the clinician may very well review the circumstances leading up to, at the time of, the patient's admission to the hospital. Going further, one would include the quality and quantity of the patient's progress during the period being evaluated. Finally, the clinician would establish the need for continued hospitalization or other treatment. This type of evaluation should be a major one (tests may or may not be given) and is more comprehensive than that found in progress or therapy notes.

Evaluation for Patient Discharge

When it is felt that a given patient has progressed sufficiently well to be discharged, it may be desirable to conduct an interview or administer a series of psychological tests. An interview may be a one-to-one type with the clinician or it may be conducted in a staffing or team level meeting. The person conducting the interview, or the person in charge of a meeting, would prepare the report. Similar to the data found in the evaluation for continued hospitalization, the discharge evaluation would review all information and intervening data from the time of the patient's admission to his anticipated discharge date. This report may very well be a summary type (to repeat details already reported in the medical records would only be redundant) and may not be much longer than one or two paragraphs. It may list recommendations for follow-up treatment such as periodic visits to an out-patient clinic, continued medication, or employment possibilities.

Chapter VI

THE DIAGNOSIS

INHERENT in the word *diagnosis* is a strong implication that the clinician has obtained all of the pertinent facts surrounding a client's case. These facts should logically lead to a diagnosis, whether or not it is an *impression, tentative, multiple,* or *final* one. Certainly no one would commit the naive sin of diagnosing a client on the basis of a snap judgment or hearsay findings. There must be some *basis* for issuing a diagnosis; if not, the diagnostic portion of the report should be omitted.

One special point worthy of mention is the question of whether or not diagnoses are necessary. A consideration to bear in mind is that diagnoses are supposedly descriptive statements about personality patterns; or, a more global view would hold that a diagnosis is a descriptive statement about a patient's totality of biological, emotional, and social functioning. Of course, the opponents of diagnostic label usage will argue against this point from every possible realm. The author feels that diagnostic labels (or whatever one wishes to call them) are expedient means by which to describe a client's physical, emotional, social, and intellectual behavior. Diagnoses are very useful *tools* of description and little more. This view holds, however, that unless the process of diagnosing clients among the different clinicians is done in a consistent manner the diagnostic rationale is far from adequate. Be that as it may, let us now assume that a client is about to be diagnosed.

THE DIAGNOSTIC PROCEDURE

The clinician should have before him all of the original information he has gathered on a given client prior to his thinking about a diagnosis. This is a general to specific approach whereby several types of data are assimilated on the client, after which these are funneled into one or two short phrases of descriptive material, namely the diagnosis. The original information would consist of interview notes, test results, therapy notes, the social history, and so forth.

Even though there may be several levels of diagnostic commitment (such as tentative or final), diagnoses will be based upon varying amounts of available facts. Figure 1 shows the process for obtaining a diagnosis on the basis of a screening interview. This method may be used by an admissions committee, a psychologist, a psychiatrist, or any other professional person. As can be seen from Figure 1, the only basis for this type of diagnostic procedure is an interview with the client or patient. This model leaves much to be desired from many standpoints. At the very least this form is highly subjective since no diagnostic aids such as laboratory tests, physical examinations, or psychological tests were used in the evaluative process. From a more comprehensive

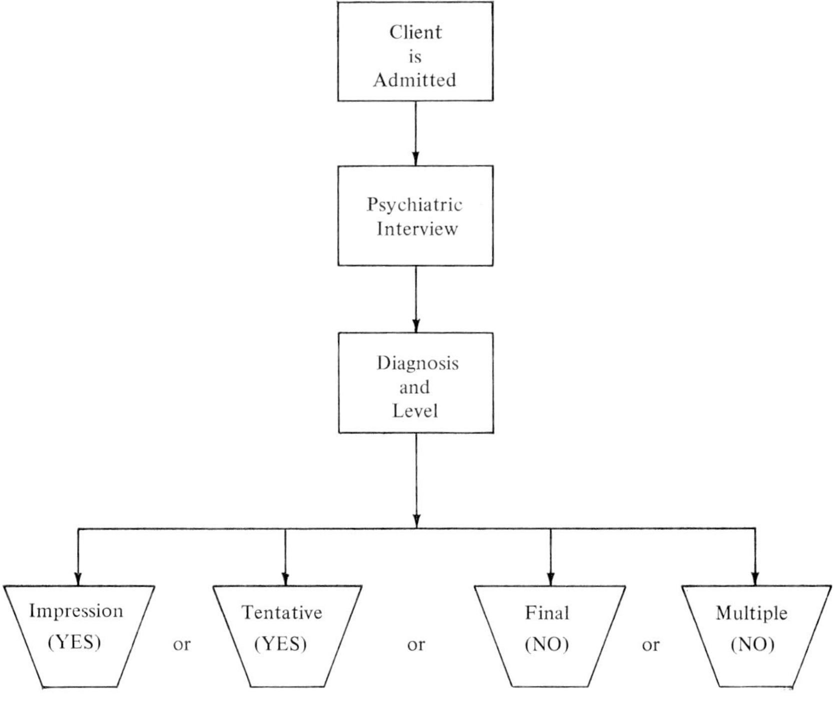

FIGURE 1. DIAGNOSTIC INTERVIEW MODEL.

evaluative standpoint, the approach in Figure 2 is more desirable, even though it may not be feasible in some situations.

Figure 2 illustrates the functions of the psychiatric interview, psychological testing, medical records, and social history data in aiding the diagnostic decision-making process. It should be emphasized that with a diagnostic model of this type one *should not* ultimately come up with either an *impression* or a *tentative* diagnosis as there are obviously too many data in support of a more definite diagnosis.

In either of Figures 1 or 2 there is an assumption that one clinician (or team) is arriving at the diagnosis. Many times one will find that a given client or patient has several diagnoses on his record as the result of on-going periods in time and different stages in his treatment program. The initial psychiatric interview will produce an *admitting diagnosis.* Later, the psychological evaluation (and subsequent test findings) will usually provide a follow-up diagnosis (which may or may not be compatible with the admitting diagnosis). On occasion a follow-up evaluation will be used to clarify an admitting diagnosis if there was some doubt as to the client's status. To exemplify, there may be a possibility of brain damage whereby a neurological examination would be requested by the clinician. Ideally, the client should only have one (at least only one *current*) diagnosis; however, this is not always the case. The reader should take further cognizance of the fact that *medical* report data are not included in these two diagnostic models *unless* the clinician is summarizing some of the physician's statements in the historical section of the psychological report. Here, medical reports are considered as *supplements* to the psychological evaluation and are the responsibility of the attending physician to prepare.

The Medical Model Diagnosis

The American Psychiatric Association distinguished between eight diagnostic areas in their first *Diagnostic and Statistical Manual* (APA, 1952). These areas were the following: a) Acute Brain Disorders, b) Chronic Brain Disorders, c) Psychotic Disorders, d) Psychophysiologic Autonomic and Visceral Disorders, e) Psychoneurotic Disorders, f) Personality Disorders, g) Tran-

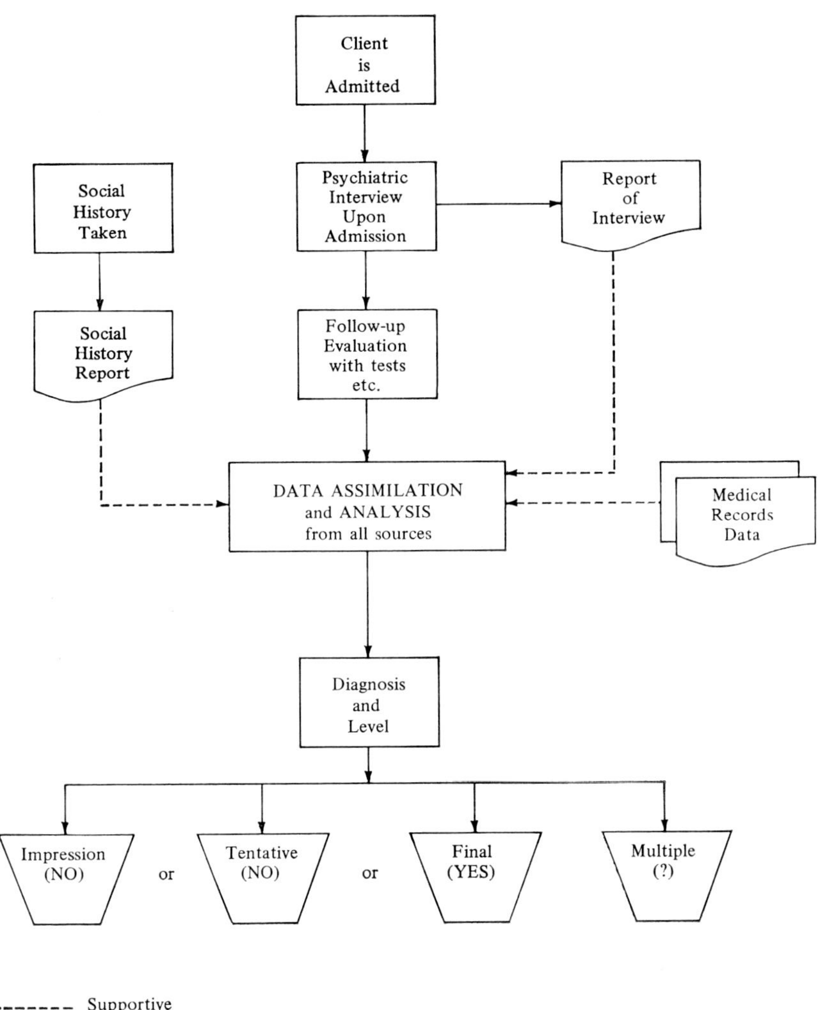

FIGURE 2. COMPREHENSIVE DIAGNOSTIC MODEL.

sient Situational Personality Disorders, and h) Mental Deficiencies. Under each of these eight major areas detailed and qualifying breakdowns were presented.

A recent revision of the American Psychiatric Association's diagnostic nomenclature (APA, 1968) lists ten major categories rather than the eight which were found in the earlier edition. In the new edition an expansion of some of the original categories is found as well as the addition of two more. The new nomenclature became "official" on July 1, 1968. These ten general categories are the following:

1. Mental Retardation.
2. Organic Brain Syndromes.
3. Psychoses not Attributed to Physical Conditions Listed Previously.
4. Neuroses.
5. Personality Disorders and Certain Other Nonpsychotic Mental Disorders.
6. Psychophysiologic Disorders.
7. Special Symptoms.
8. Transient Situational Disturbances.
9. Behavioral Disorders of Childhood and Adolescence.
10. Conditions Without Manifest Psychiatric Disorder and Nonspecific Conditions.

An eleventh category (Non-Diagnostic Terms for Administrative Use) is for administrative use and is not a diagnostic category per se.

The American Psychiatric Association's *Diagnostic and Statistical Manual* points out the importance of diagnostic compatibility in that one should not violate diagnostic *rules*. For example, a patient should not be diagnosed as "Anxiety reaction (psychoneurosis) with paranoia (psychosis)." One cannot be *both* psychoneurotic *and* psychotic at the same time! On the other hand, one *can* diagnose a patient as "Mental retardation, severe, with psychotic reaction." Again, this brings one to the subject of *primary* and *secondary* diagnoses.

Figure 3 illustrates the American Psychiatric Association's nomenclature *in toto*. A form such as this can be used as a worksheet if desired. Both the old and the new nomenclatures present a strong medical model approach; however, the new nomenclature does acknowledge several nonmedical entities. In a supportive article, Spitzer and Wilson (1968) noted that in particular, the new category, "Conditions without manifest psychiatric disorder and nonspecific conditions," should have usefulness in the area of applied forensic psychiatry. Furthermore, the new

<table>
<tr><td>Patient's last name   first</td><td>Identification number</td><td>Physician</td><td>Date (month, day, year)</td></tr>
</table>

Instructions: Indicate the patient's diagnosis by placing a heavy mark in the box next to the appropriate diagnosis.

MENTAL RETARDATION
- ☐ 310.   Borderline
- ☐ 311.   Mild
- ☐ 312.   Moderate
- ☐ 313.   Severe
- ☐ 314.   Profound
- ☐ 315.   Unspecified

With each: Following or associated with
- ☐ .0   Infection or intoxication
- ☐ .1   Trauma or physical agent
- ☐ .2   Disorders of metabolism, growth or nutrition
- ☐ .3   Gross brain disease (postnatal)
- ☐ .4   Unknown prenatal influence
- ☐ .5   Chromosomal abnormality
- ☐ .6   Prematurity
- ☐ .7   Major psychiatric disorder
- ☐ .8   Psycho-social (environmental) deprivation
- ☐ .9   Other condition

II   ORGANIC BRAIN SYNDROMES (OBS)
A   PSYCHOSES
Senile and pre-senile dementia
- ☐ 290.0   Senile dementia
- ☐ 290.1   Pre-senile dementia

Alcoholic psychosis
- ☐ 291.0   Delirium tremens
- ☐ 291.1   Korsakov's psychosis
- ☐ 291.2   Other alcoholic hallucinosis
- ☐ 291.3   Alcohol paranoid state
- ☐ 291.4*   Acute alcohol intoxication*
- ☐ 291.5*   Alcoholic deterioration*
- ☐ 291.6*   Pathological intoxication*
- ☐ 291.9   Other alcoholic psychosis

Psychosis associated with intracranial infection
- ☐ 292.0   General paralysis
- ☐ 292.1   Syphilis of central nervous system
- ☐ 292.2   Epidemic encephalitis
- ☐ 292.3   Other and unspecified encephalitis
- ☐ 292.9   Other intracranial infection

Psychosis associated with other cerebral condition
- ☐ 293.0   Cerebral arteriosclerosis
- ☐ 293.1   Other cerebrovascular disturbance
- ☐ 293.2   Epilepsy
- ☐ 293.3   Intracranial neoplasm
- ☐ 293.4   Degenerative disease of the CNS
- ☐ 293.5   Brain trauma
- ☐ 293.9   Other cerebral condition

Psychosis associated with other physical condition
- ☐ 294.0   Endocrine disorder
- ☐ 294.1   Metabolic and nutritional disorder
- ☐ 294.2   Systemic infection
- ☐ 294.3   Drug or poison intoxication (other than alcohol)
- ☐ 294.4   Childbirth
- ☐ 294.8   Other and unspecified physical condition

B   NON-PSYCHOTIC OBS
- ☐ 309.0   Intracranial infection
- ☐ 309.13*   Alcohol* (simple drunkenness)
- ☐ 309.14*   Other drug, poison or systemic intoxication*
- ☐ 309.2   Brain trauma
- ☐ 309.3   Circulatory disturbance
- ☐ 309.4   Epilepsy
- ☐ 309.5   Disturbance of metabolism, growth, or nutrition
- ☐ 309.6   Senile or pre-senile brain disease
- ☐ 309.7   Intracranial neoplasm
- ☐ 309.8   Degenerative disease of the CNS
- ☐ 309.9   Other physical condition

* Categories added to ICD-8 for use in U.S. only.

III   PSYCHOSES NOT ATTRIBUTED TO PHYSICAL CONDITIONS LISTED PREVIOUSLY
Schizophrenia
- ☐ 295.0   Simple
- ☐ 295.1   Hebephrenic
- ☐ 295.2   Catatonic
- ☐ 295.23*   Catatonic type, excited*
- ☐ 295.24*   Catatonic type, withdrawn*
- ☐ 295.3   Paranoid
- ☐ 295.4   Acute schizophrenic episode
- ☐ 295.5   Latent
- ☐ 295.6   Residual
- ☐ 295.7   Schizo-affective
- ☐ 295.73*   Schizo-affective, excited*
- ☐ 295.74*   Schizo-affective, depressed*
- ☐ 295.8*   Childhood*
- ☐ 295.90*   Chronic undifferentiated*
- ☐ 295.99*   Other schizophrenia*

Major affective disorders
- ☐ 296.0   Involutional melancholia
- ☐ 296.1   Manic-depressive illness, manic
- ☐ 296.2   Manic-depressive illness, depressed
- ☐ 296.3   Manic-depressive illness, circular
- ☐ 296.33*   Manic-depressive, circular, manic*
- ☐ 296.34*   Manic-depressive, circular, depressed*
- ☐ 296.8   Other major affective disorder

Paranoid states
- ☐ 297.0   Paranoia
- ☐ 297.1   Involutional paranoid state
- ☐ 297.9   Other paranoid state

Other psychoses
- ☐ 298.0   Psychotic depressive reaction

IV   NEUROSES
- ☐ 300.0   Anxiety
- ☐ 300.1   Hysterical
- ☐ 300.13*   Hysterical, conversion type*
- ☐ 300.14*   Hysterical, dissociative type*
- ☐ 300.2   Phobic
- ☐ 300.3   Obsessive compulsive
- ☐ 300.4   Depressive
- ☐ 300.5   Neurasthenic
- ☐ 300.6   Depersonalization
- ☐ 300.7   Hypochondriacal
- ☐ 300.8   Other neurosis

V   PERSONALITY DISORDERS AND CERTAIN OTHER NON-PSYCHOTIC MENTAL DISORDERS
Personality disorders
- ☐ 301.0   Paranoid
- ☐ 301.1   Cyclothymic
- ☐ 301.2   Schizoid
- ☐ 301.3   Explosive
- ☐ 301.4   Obsessive compulsive
- ☐ 301.5   Hysterical
- ☐ 301.6   Asthenic
- ☐ 301.7   Antisocial
- ☐ 301.81*   Passive-aggressive*
- ☐ 301.82*   Inadequate*
- ☐ 301.89*   Other specified types*

Sexual deviation
- ☐ 302.0   Homosexuality
- ☐ 302.1   Fetishism
- ☐ 302.2   Pedophilia
- ☐ 302.3   Transvestitism
- ☐ 302.4   Exhibitionism
- ☐ 302.5*   Voyeurism*
- ☐ 302.6*   Sadism*
- ☐ 302.7*   Masochism*
- ☐ 302.8   Other sexual deviation

Alcoholism
- ☐ 303.0   Episodic excessive drinking
- ☐ 303.1   Habitual excessive drinking
- ☐ 303.2   Alcohol addiction
- ☐ 303.9   Other alcoholism

Drug dependence
- ☐ 304.0   Opium, opium alkaloids and their derivatives
- ☐ 304.1   Synthetic analgesics with morphine-like effects
- ☐ 304.2   Barbiturates
- ☐ 304.3   Other hypnotics and sedatives or "tranquilizers"
- ☐ 304.4   Cocaine
- ☐ 304.5   Cannabis sativa (hashish, marihuana)
- ☐ 304.6   Other psycho-stimulants
- ☐ 304.7   Hallucinogens
- ☐ 304.8   Other drug dependence

VI   PSYCHOPHYSIOLOGIC DISORDERS
- ☐ 305.0   Skin
- ☐ 305.1   Musculoskeletal
- ☐ 305.2   Respiratory
- ☐ 305.3   Cardiovascular
- ☐ 305.4   Hemic and lymphatic
- ☐ 305.5   Gastro-intestinal
- ☐ 305.6   Genito-urinary
- ☐ 305.7   Endocrine
- ☐ 305.8   Organ of special sense
- ☐ 305.9   Other type

VII   SPECIAL SYMPTOMS
- ☐ 306.0   Speech disturbance
- ☐ 306.1   Specific learning disturbance
- ☐ 306.2   Tic
- ☐ 306.3   Other psychomotor disorder
- ☐ 306.4   Disorders of sleep
- ☐ 306.5   Feeding disturbance
- ☐ 306.6   Enuresis
- ☐ 306.7   Encopresis
- ☐ 306.8   Cephalalgia
- ☐ 306.9   Other special symptom

VIII   TRANSIENT SITUATIONAL DISTURBANCES
- ☐ 307.0*   Adjustment reaction of infancy*
- ☐ 307.1*   Adjustment reaction of childhood*
- ☐ 307.2*   Adjustment reaction of adolescence*
- ☐ 307.3*   Adjustment reaction of adult life*
- ☐ 307.4*   Adjustment reaction of late life*

IX   BEHAVIOR DISORDERS OF CHILD-HOOD AND ADOLESCENCE
- ☐ 308.0*   Hyperkinetic reaction*
- ☐ 308.1*   Withdrawing reaction*
- ☐ 308.2*   Overanxious reaction*
- ☐ 308.3*   Runaway reaction*
- ☐ 308.4*   Unsocialized aggressive reaction*
- ☐ 308.5*   Group delinquent reaction*
- ☐ 308.9*   Other reaction*

X   CONDITIONS WITHOUT MANIFEST PSYCHIATRIC DISORDER AND NON-SPECIFIC CONDITIONS
Social maladjustment without manifest psychiatric disorder
- ☐ 316.0*   Marital maladjustment*
- ☐ 316.1*   Social maladjustment*
- ☐ 316.2*   Occupational maladjustment*
- ☐ 316.3*   Dyssocial behavior*
- ☐ 316.9*   Other social maladjustment*

Non-specific conditions
- ☐ 317*   Non-specific conditions*

No Mental Disorder
- ☐ 318*   No mental disorder*

XI   NON-DIAGNOSTIC TERMS FOR ADMINISTRATIVE USE
- ☐ 319.0*   Diagnosis deferred*
- ☐ 319.1*   Boarder*
- ☐ 319.2*   Experiment only*
- ☐ 319.3*   Other*

FIFTH DIGIT QUALIFYING PHRASES

Section II
- ☐ .X1   Acute
- ☐ .X2   Chronic

Section III
- ☐ .X6   Not psychotic now

Sections IV through IX
- ☐ .X6   Mild
- ☐ .X7   Moderate
- ☐ .X8   Severe

All disorders
- ☐ .X5   In remission

FIGURE 3. DIAGNOSTIC NOMENCLATURE.

nomenclature will make the United States' classification system more compatible with the four-digit international classification code system of psychiatric disorders (APA, 1968).

The Behavioral Model Diagnosis

There has been a tradition for many years for most psychologists, psychiatrists, and others to diagnose patients and clients in terms of medically-oriented labels, such as "schizophrenia," "chronic brain syndrome," and others. However, these labels tell the reader nothing if he is not already familiar with the underlying rationale for the given label. In effect, the label tends to *describe* a syndrome with *implied* behavior specificity. This is where a diagnosis based on manifest behavioral indices might be more effective.

Proponents of the *behavior modification* approach of therapeutic intervention have, for several years, been working toward a system of behavioral diagnosis. This approach is based upon Skinnerian types of reinforcement or operant contingencies which basically purport a) to identify environmental phenomena which "cause" a given behavior; b) to identify the manifest, resultant behavior; c) to ascertain the intrinsic and extrinsic reinforcers of a given behavior; and d) to define contingencies which can be used to control (shape) this behavior. There is much less emphasis upon the medical and analytic constructs of one's personality. To date, there has been no systematized nomenclature developed (equivalent to the APA system) for a behavioral diagnostic framework. Much of the present *diagnosing* is done on an individual level by which the behavior modificationist identifies and clarifies manifest patient behaviors which need to be changed. Subsequent treatment programming is designed to increase or decrease a given behavior or behavior system, if not the patient's physical environment.

Primary and Secondary Diagnoses

The *primary* diagnosis is thought of as the single, most outstanding feature of the client's physical and psychological behavior. Usually, the reason for the client's admission to treatment is the primary diagnosis (unless of course a follow-up evaluation reveals information to the contrary as in the case of brain damage, et cetera). If known at the time of admission, a primary diagnosis would be within one of ten major APA diagnostic areas. Additionally, the clinician would indicate the *specificity* of the diagnostic area such as "Schizophrenic reaction, catatonic type, excited" (this is, of course, a psychotic disorder).

The *secondary* diagnosis is an *additive* statement to the primary diagnosis. This form is used when even further clarification of the patient's problem is needed. The secondary diagnosis is usually preceded by the preposition, *with.* An example, would be, "Mental retardation, severe, *with* gross brain disease." The phrase, *with* gross brain disease, is the secondary diagnosis. It is preferable to use a single diagnosis with a primary and a secondary clause instead of using a multiple diagnosis; however, there are exceptions when multiple diagnoses are expedient. These exceptions will be discussed later.

A *tertiary* feature of diagnoses is that of the *qualifying phrase* within a primary diagnosis. Here one finds the specific type of dysfunction within the general diagnostic category. In the case of mental retardation, for example, the *intensity* of the condition, such as "mild," "moderate," or "severe" would be the qualifier. Another example of a qualifying phrase would be, "Personality disorder, *antisocial type.*" The qualifier follows a *comma* in the primary clause of the diagnosis—the secondary clause follows the preposition, *with.* Diagnoses can at times be ambiguous enough without the clinician leaving out portions of the diagnostic statement or phrase. It is always a good idea to be as specific as your evaluative data will allow.

Diagnostic Levels

Diagnostic Impression

An impression diagnosis is one whereby the clinician cannot be sufficiently sure of the client's mental status to warrant a final or a multiple diagnosis. A diagnostic impression may be stated when the results of a preliminary interview with the client *seem* to classify him one way or another. The client may create an *impression* of mental retardation, brain damage, or schizophrenia.

However, further evaluation (interviews and testing) are frequently needed for the clinician to be more certain of a diagnosis. A familiar example is the commonplace situation where one makes a "first impression" judgment of a person you meet for the first time. One's first impression may very well turn out to be in error after being around this person for a time. The same can be true of the *diagnostic impression*. It is a first-time judgment of a client's mental status. The diagnostic impression should always be considered as a *temporary* diagnosis until additional facts on the client have been obtained.

Tentative Diagnosis

The tentative diagnosis is quite similar to the diagnostic impression in that it is based on limited data on a client. One can also consider the tentative diagnosis as the clinician's admittance that a follow-up evaluation and subsequent diagnosis should be made. For the most part, both impression and tentative diagnoses are synonymous diagnostic levels; they are temporary and by no means final.

Final Diagnosis

When speaking of diagnoses one may feel that it is facetious to consider a final (or absolute) psychological diagnosis. For example, after the administration of an intelligence test one can be reasonably certain (or absolute) that a client *is* or *is not* mentally retarded. Similarly, one may be either psychotic, prepsychotic, or psychotic. On a psychiatric interview the clinician may *suspect* brain damage when a client has a poor memory, short attention span, and has an unsteady gait; thus, a diagnostic *impression* of "Organic brain syndrome, nonpsychotic, associated with brain trauma" might be given if no symptoms of emotional pathology were present. Or, a diagnosis of "possible brain syndrome" might be offered. In either example a follow-up evaluation would be justified in order to arrive at a final diagnosis. On a follow-up evaluation a *final* diagnosis of "Organic brain syndrome, associated with intracranial neoplasm" might be given. When not otherwise qualified, the singular term, "diagnosis," will usually refer to a final diagnosis. Another point to keep in mind is that even though psychological phenomena are not absolute in the same sense that the laws of physics are, they are as absolute as possible under the cognitive realm. One can be a great deal more final in their diagnosis of mental retardation or brain damage than in the functional neuroses and psychoses. This is mainly due to the problem of descriptive semantics.

Multiple Diagnoses

As previously illustrated in Figures 1 and 2, a multiple diagnosis is one of four possible diagnostic levels. However, if at all possible, more than one diagnosis for a client on a given report should be avoided. The reason is simple—the reader of the report would still have doubts about what the diagnosis would be. A choice between diagnoses must be made if the reader is to have a single diagnostic indicator for statistical or other reasons. It goes without saying that when a clinician makes more than one diagnosis on a client on the same report, a lack of specificity results. A more desirable approach is to use a *differential diagnosis* section which leads to a single diagnostic index. In a differential diagnosis one considers the rationale for each of two (or even three) diagnoses and then arrives at a single diagnostic indicator which best describes the client's status. The process is a form of diagnostic compromise.

Many times the clinician can use the technique of primary and secondary diagnostic statements in order to avoid a multiple diagnosis. An example of a multiple diagnosis which should be in primary-secondary form is the following:

Example A
1. Mental retardation, mild.
2. Psychotic reaction.

The primary-secondary form is more suitable and is stated as, "Mental retardation, mild, with major psychiatric disorder." Note that the *organic* component of the diagnosis (mental retardation) is stated as the primary condition while the emotional factor is the secondary condition. On the other hand, an appropriate use of a multiple diagnosis might be the following:

Example B
1. Personality disorder, explosive type.
2. Transient situational disturbance, adjustment reaction of adolescence.

In Example B, the clinician had doubt as to the diagnosis best describing the client's behavior; thus, a multiple diagnosis seemed to be justified. Another case where a multiple diagnosis might be used is the following:

Example C
1. Schizophrenic reaction, schizo-affective, depressed type.
2. Behavior disorder of adolescence, withdrawing reaction.

Again, the client's symptomology and history were sufficiently obscure so as to prevent him from obtaining a more refined level of diagnostic certainty. It should be pointed out that in most circumstances the diagnostician will be able to decide on a single diagnosis; but, occasionally the symptoms may be rather obscure.

The aforementioned two examples, B and C, of multiple diagnoses were composed of two separate *groups* of diagnoses; that is, they crossed two of the ten major APA diagnostic classification areas. Sometimes, a more legitimate multiple diagnosis may come from within *one* diagnostic group, such as the following:

Example D
1. Special symptom reaction, *speech disturbance.*
2. Special symptom reaction, *enuresis.*

With Example D, both problems were present; and, diagnostic etiquette disallows combining both in a single statement since each has separate APA code numbers, *viz.* 306.0 and 306.6, respectively. At the very least, the APA coding procedure creates a mechanical problem in the combining of diagnostic areas.

Multiple diagnoses can result within a single report on a client when a) the clinician has conflicting data; b) the client's record displays more than one definite syndromatic pattern; and c) the clinician is unable to decide on one single diagnosis due to his ineptness. It is hoped that the reader will never have to use the third item.

Diagnostic Summary

On occasion the clinical diagnosis in APA terminology may not be desirable (as in the case where the clinician does not wish to affix a "label" on a client). Therefore, a device known as the *diagnostic summary* may be used. This is a summary statement in symptomatic or descriptive terms, illustrated by the following example:

Example E
The client presents a history of severe loss of contact with reality, being circumscribed with severe disorientation to time, place, and person. His ideation contains fragmented thought processes and delusions of persecution of a mild degree.

In Example E, the diagnostic label, if used, would probably be, "Schizophrenic reaction, chronic undifferentiated type."

A diagnostic summary statement would be useful on reports going to any person who would tend to misinterpret a label. For example, the school guidance counselor may find a diagnostic summary approach useful on reports going to lay readers. Additionally, any clinician may elect to used this approach, *followed* by a clinical (label) diagnosis. The ultimate choice is left up to the clinician, and organizational and State policies as to which diagnostic form to use.

A word of caution is given in the use of diagnoses. It is quite easy for one to have preconceived notions about a client's diagnosis prior to an evaluation of data on the client. A personal example is cited. The author was once asked to conduct a psychological evaluation on a client. For some reason the author was told that the client was believed to exhibit sociopathic behavior. A psychological evaluation followed. As predicted, patterns of sociopathy were derived from the client's responses. Whether or not the author's prior knowledge of a possible diagnostic category actually influenced the evaluative procedures will never definitely be known. The moral of this example is, *let the record speak for itself.* Arrive at a diagnosis that is based on the information received from the client, the psychometric results, the medical history, and the social history. If diagnoses must be compared, first arrive at *your* diagnosis and then compare it with other clinician's views or diagnoses, but *post facto.*

Chapter VII

THE SOCIAL HISTORY STATEMENT

WITHIN THE REALM of psychological report writing is often found a description of a client's behavior prior to his out-patient or in-patient treatment. Additionally, and quite important, are the factors which shape the client's family and other primary group involvements, prior to or concurrent with treatment. This is where the *social history statement* plays a very significant part in the psychological report.

A distinction should be made between the client's comprehensive social history (usually two or more pages) taken by the social worker, and a *summary* of the social history data found in the psychological report. In the latter situation the clinician may either a) obtain the historical data first-hand, or b) excerpt the pertinent data from a previously prepared social history. Generally, the social history statement in a psychological report should not exceed one-half of a page in the final typed psychological report.

Usually, a social history per se and the inclusion of social history data in the psychological report are two separate items. Analogous to this is where the "history and physical" statement in a physician's report comprises only a portion of the over-all medical examination report. Similarly, the social history statement forms only a part of the complete psychological examination.

THE COMPLETE SOCIAL HISTORY

The social worker is usually the one who prepares the lengthy social history on a client. For the most part, the social worker will thoroughly investigate the client's family, developmental, medical, religious, employment, educational, and leisure-time activities. From these data he is then able to write a comprehensive *social history*. These data may come from an interview with the client, the family, visits in the client's home, as well as talks with the client's friends, his clergyman, the family physician, or from other persons involved in the case. The historical information on the client can be obtained by talking with these persons in the social worker's office, by sending out questionnaires, or by going out in the field. If the client has received previous psychiatric treatment, the social worker may consult previous medical records, including any interim social histories, for the necessary information. For the most part, the social history will be obtained from the immediate family of the patient, since the patient may be unable (or unwilling) to submit accurate information of this nature to the interviewer.

The significance of the social history will have different meanings for different clinicians. The person who is psychoanalytically oriented may eagerly peruse the social history for any indices of oedipal attachments, sibling rivalries, traumatic toilet-training experiences, and so forth. Social psychologists may review the history for any peer-group conflicts, work experiences, family interactions, and sociopersonal learning experiences. Another therapist may disregard the past and concentrate only on the client's immediate problem behavior, displayed at the time of the patient's admission to the hospital or clinic. Suffice to say that the social history can be used by each clinician in the manner in which he feels is expedient in order to shed light on the nature of the client's conflicts and manifest problem behavior.

THE SOCIAL HISTORY STATEMENT

Nearly all psychological reports contain some statement (or paragraph) of an historic, social nature on each client. More typically, these comments will be used as a partial explanation for the client's hospitalization or out-patient visits. On the other hand, the social history provides a reference point by which to compare future behavioral and cognitive change.

Comments pertaining to the client's immediate or distant social past will usually follow a statement explaining the reason for the psychological evaluation and subsequent report. A sample report sequence might be the following:

1. Identifying data.
2. Reason for referral.
3. *Social history statement.*
4. Interview data.
5. Psychometric results.
6. Et cetera.

As heretofore stated, the social history statement will include comments on the client's developmental history, work history, history of emotional symptoms, religious activities, and the like.

Content of the Social History Statement

The best social history statement will be as brief and as concise as possible without omitting essential details. An extensive, narrrative history statement of several pages has no place in the body of the routine psychological report. The preparation of a more detailed report is the function of the social worker. A sketchy history which presents information gaps, contradictions, unaccounted for periods of time, and highly biased details is not desirable either. Nevertheless, reports of this nature will occur from time to time, despite the clinician's skill at gleaning social history information from the informants. Still, some historical data are better than none at all.

The general content of the social history statement will usually include several areas of information. *Identifying data* (part of which may appear in the identification portion of the psychological report) includes the patient's name, age, sex, education, marital status, family structure, religious affiliation, financial status (optional), occupation, and employment trends. Second, is the patient's *developmental chronology* which includes such information as the patient's birth (whether routine or complicated), position in the family (only child, youngest, etc.), toilet training experiences, preschool education and orientation, school educational and emotional experiences and adjustments, childhood diseases and accidents, extracurricular experiences and degrees of success, family relations and interactions, and any other developmental areas of importance. Third, the patient's *pre-admission status* is reviewed. Here, the manifest physical, social, and emotional conditions of the patient at the time of (and immediately before) his out-patient or in-patient admission are discussed.

Furthermore, the circumstances which led the patient to treatment are discussed. That is, what were the obvious physical, social, or emotional behaviors which the patient elicited thereby indicating his need for treatment? Was he hostile and aggressive, unmanageable, suicidal, homicidal, irresponsible, highly irrational or what? Did he seek mental treatment voluntarily or did the court order his confinement as the result of a physician's certificate being issued? These are only a few of the many possible questions the clinician may investigate.

The reader will recall from Chapters II and III that the identifying data on a client are given only once. Therefore, a restatement of this information in the social history section of the psychological report would be superfluous.

An example of a summary social history statement in a psychological report appears in Case No. 1.

Case No. 1

This forty-five-year-old white married female was admitted to the hospital under the direction of a Court order resulting from the issuance of a physician's certificate.

She has a high school education and has worked as a waitress for several years. She has no previous history of mental illness, even though both of her parents had been institutionalized the last few years of their lives. The patient has been married for 25 years and has three children, aged 5, 10, and 22. Before her admission, she seemingly became quite aggressive, delusional, and felt that electrical impulses were controlling her behavior. Before her admission, she was very unmanageable and uncooperative at home.

Obviously, this history statement in a psychological report leaves much to be desired. It tells very little about the patient's past. A better written and more descriptive social history statement would be written as shown in Case No. 2.

Case No. 2

This forty-five-year-old white married female was admitted to the hospital under the direction of a Court order resulting from the issuance of a physician's certificate.

She has a twelfth grade education, is of the protestant religion, and comes from a low income level family of seven (she has four brothers, all living). She had an uneventful birth, had experienced the usual childhood illnesses, and was the youngest of the five children. She had engaged in a few extracurricular school activities and made low average grades.

As a child, the patient was reported as getting along well with her family and school peers, despite her tendency toward introversive and shy behavior. When she was ten years old her parents were divorced and she subsequently lived with her father until her marriage at age sixteen to a local boy. Up until this admission, she had never been treated for mental illness, even though both of her parents had received extensive psychiatric care for several years until the time of their death in an automobile accident two years ago.

The patient reports she has been happily married for twenty-five years (confirmed by her husband) and has three boys, aged 5, 10, and 22.

At the time of her admission, she appeared unkempt in dress and was very confused. It was related by the husband that the patient had become very aggressive, unmanageable, and rather uncooperative at home (she would severely spank her youngest child with little provocation) and felt that external forces (electromagnetic waves from the television) were controlling her thoughts and behavior. Her husband reported that she had lost interest in sexual activities for the past several months.

Case No. 2 is a great deal more informative (even though above average in desirable length) than the first. A statement such as this can be very useful in either the patient's initial psychiatric evaluation on admission (if available to the admitting clinician) or on a follow-up psychological examination. Functionally, the social history statement in Case No. 2, could serve as the identifying, purpose or reason, and social history statement sections of a given psychological report. In effect, the exact placement of the social history statement in the psychological report would depend upon the contents of the statement. Additionally, if subheadings are used in the overall report, then the contents of a statement such as in Case No. 2 would probably be dispersed throughout two or three of these subheading areas.

Chapter VIII

THE PSYCHIATRIC EXAMINATION

THE PSYCHIATRIC EXAMINATION is an important device to use in diagnosis and treatment programming of the patient. It is usually the initial patient evaluation which the clinician conducts and precedes any psychological testing activities. As soon as a client or patient is admitted to a treatment facility, he is ordinarily given this interview by the psychologist, psychiatrist, or other clinician. The psychiatric examination, for example, may also be called an intake interview, an initial screening evaluation, or a staffing interview. Even though a therapeutic contact, such as an individual or group psychotherapy session may be called an "interview," the psychiatric examination carries the connotation of being an evaluative or a diagnostic device.

GENERAL CONSIDERATIONS

During the psychiatric examination the clinician attempts to investigate several major areas of the client's functioning. One area concerns the *how* and *why* of the patient's admission to the treatment facility. That is, what were the major nonintegrative behaviors that the person exhibited; and, did he seek treatment voluntarily or was he committed by a court? Next, what is the patient's social history? In what ways was he behaving prior to his coming for treatment? These social phenomena would probably include the client's dealings with his immediate family, friends, employer, and others in the community. Another broad area of concern is the patient's present social, emotional, physical, and behavioral functioning, both qualitatively and quantitatively. These three broad areas are only general realms by which the clinician can structure his interviewing of the patient; that is, structure from the standpoint of what you wish to find out about the client in order to plan his treatment program.

Sullivan (1954) mentions that the psychiatric interview, over one or more sessions, may last from one to perhaps six hours. It is felt that this type of interview would not be suitable for the routine psychiatric examination in discussion here. Granted, several hours of interviewing could probably lead to a very detailed and comprehensive analysis of one's client. However, the primary objective of the psychiatric examination is to obtain an estimate of the client's present mental status for diagnostic and treatment programming purposes, and not that of brief psychoanalysis. More practically, the psychiatric examination can be conducted in from fifteen to sixty minutes, depending upon the expertise of the clinician and the patient's cooperation. Where the diagnostic caseload and patient intake schedules are heavy, brief but complete interviews will be quite practical.

In order to write a psychiatric examination report, based on first-hand observations, the clinician should obtain the desired information from the client himself. If the client is found to be uncooperative, nontalkative, heavily sedated, or physiologically mute or deaf, then the clinician must alter his interview approach quite drastically during the interview session. When little verbal information can be withdrawn from the client, additional qualitative and quantitative emotional inferences must be made. On the other hand, information obtained from the client's family and friends, or any other involved persons can be used for supplementing the report.

If the clinician is to conduct a worthwhile psychiatric examination, as many factors as possible which contribute to the client's global functioning should be kept in mind. The clinician should sharpen his skills at *observing* the *physical, emotional, social,* and *intellectual* levels of his client's functioning. Accurate and thorough observations will enable one to develop a report that will be both informative and useful to the potential reader.

The psychiatric examination interview should be conducted by the same clinician who plans to write the report—this goes along with the *first-hand observation* criteria of successful report writing which has been mentioned earlier.

Sometimes, circumstances will develop whereby the clinician must prepare a *post facto* report; however, this is extremely undesirable. If the clinician is called upon for this type of an examination, then the clinician-client relationship cannot be met. When this situation does exist, one must review any previous records (which may or may not be completely accurate) that are available on the *ex*-client, consult with other clinicians who have been in contact with the client, and finally formulate a report based on third-party criteria. Any *post facto* report will at best be the clinician's educated guess based on hearsay evidence and consensus of third-party observations (only an *impression* diagnosis would be appropriate here, unless medical or psychological test results specified a given condition). Finally, a *post facto* report may be *illegal!*

The pschiatric interview should be conducted so that many areas of functioning are elicited. The interviewer should concentrate on the global physical, emotional, behavioral, social, and intellectual processes of his client. This interview should be primarily a fact-finding process with emphasis on the client's *present mental status.* The thorough interview should have treatment implications in view as well as a basis for specific treatment recommendations for the therapists to follow.

The direction of the psychiatric examination should not be solely governed by the clinician's own therapeutic and theoretical orientation and inculcate biases. One could not write an effective report if only reinforcement contingencies, oedipal complexes, or religious problems are of primary concern to the interviewer. Similarly, too much emphasis upon past developmental phenomena as well as over emphasis upon present levels of functioning can present problems. The writer of a report should also avoid using an extreme nondirective interview approach which would possibly lead to an omission of much factual and relevant data. Furthermore, the psychiatric examination should not be the basis for a *theoretical* dissertation of the client's intrapsychic personality or his behavioral adaptations to his environment. It should be a presentation of facts and circumstances which are as concrete and as definitive as possible, thereby efficiently describing the client's over-all level of functioning.

In effect, the psychiatric examination will depend upon the training, experience, and therapeutic orientation of the interviewer despite any idealized bias-free reporting procedures. Reports with different views will evolve from general practitioners, psychiatrists, clinical psychologists, guidance counselors, and social workers. Obviously, no one except a physician who is licensed to practice medicine could prescribe medication and related medical treatments; therefore, reports made by physicians may very well assume a different orientation than those prepared by nonmedical practitioners.

The psychologist may wonder whether or not he should take verbatim notes during the actual interview. This will ultimately depend upon his own preferences. Sullivan (1954) felt that note-taking during the interview tended to interfere with the client-therapist interpersonal interaction process. He further felt that the interviewer should attend more to the verbal content and feeling tone, as well as to the overt physical emotions elicited by the client, than to the clerical process. Sullivan did feel, however, that note-taking may be of benefit with clients who tend to produce little verbal information. If certain responses which the client gives seem to be especially significant, accurate and verbatim notes may be quite important for compiling the written report. The verbal productions of schizophrenics or depressives, for example, may be quite important to record in this manner. Furthermore, verbatim records of clients who indicate strong, overt hostile-aggressive trends (especially those statements with homicidal or suicidal implications) may be the basis for security or continued hospitalization decisions.

In some cases the verbatim recordings of a client's responses may be admissible as evidence in some litigation proceedings. However, there are a number of contradictions as to what type of *evidence* may be considered factual in the courts. Most authorities seem to feel that psychiatric evidence is somewhat hearsay when compared to other types of three-dimensional, tangible, and concrete evidence. While most courts do not seem to admit psychiatric findings as evidence in the generic sense of the word, they may very well receive it within the framework of *expert testimony*. This legal area will be discussed in greater detail in Chapter XIV.

Noyes and Kolb (1963), as do many other writers, take a medical model approach to the psychiatric examination. They feel that one must obtain a concise historical account of the client's functioning within a problem-centered framework. On the other hand, the client's approach to his problems-in-living as they relate to the here and now behavior may be of much greater importance.

The psychiatric history and the psychiatric examination should include several important points. The *reason* for the client's consultation or commitment to the hospital or clinic is of primary importance. A verbatim statement of the client's manifest problem area should be obtained. The client's statement should be as detailed as possible. If this information cannot be obtained from the client personally, then a statement should be sought from a third party.

A full account of the symptomology leading to the client's present illness or behavioral problem should be outlined. Any significant environmental stressors which seemed to have precipitated his unconventional behavior should also be identified. Comments on the client's family history, his previous illnesses, and social interactions should similarly be made.

During the interview, the client's general appearance, attitude, stream of consciousness, mood, expressive behavior, thought processes, mental trend, perceptions, memory, general information about his environment, judgment, and insight should be noted (Noyes and Kolb, 1963, pp. 115-127). These observations will prove to be of great help when the final report is being written. During the interview-examination the clinician should keep his future report in mind so that he will reduce his chances for overlooking meaningful information.

CONTENT OF THE PSYCHIATRIC EXAMINATION

Five major areas of the client's functioning should be investigated during the psychiatric examination. These areas are the following: a) general identifying information; b) the developmental history; c) the physical history and current status; d) mental status; and e) the client's social behavior.

General Identifying Information

This area includes that information which is necessary in order to identify the client and to ascertain the nature and reason for his coming for treatment. The points that should be covered on all patients are:

1. Client's name, usual place of residence, age, sex, marital status, educational level, occupation, religious affiliation, race, and (optional) names of relatives or guardians.
2. Date and type of admission (voluntary, emergency, court order, etc.).
3. Names of any referring agencies (where applicable, such as school counselors, penal institutions, private physicians, welfare agencies, etc.).
4. Circumstances at admission (voluntarily entered facility, handcuffed, in ambulance, with friends, etc.).
5. Problem or reason for seeking treatment (from patient or referrants).

Development History

Here, the clinician will want to obtain some historical data on the client's childhood rearing, learning experiences, physical maturation, and personality development. The nature and extent of the information obtained will depend upon the therapeutic orientation of the interviewer. However, all therapists should attempt to make some comments on each of the following points.

1. Age when the client began to walk, talk, and was toilet-trained.
2. Preschool learning and socialization experiences.
3. School experiences (academic grades, learning problems, extracurricular activities, peer-relations, etc.).
4. Emotional development.
5. Physical history (see physical history section).

Physical History and Current Status

Any physiological factors which may have contributed to physical, emotional, intellectual, or social problems would be indicated as the following.

History

1. Birth experience (natural or caesarean, complications, etc.).
2. Childhood diseases, acute or chronic.

3. Accidents, automobile or other, resulting in head injuries, loss of limbs, etc.
4. Special medical problems (diabetes, rheumatic heart disease, etc.).
5. Epilepsy or similar convulsive disorders.
6. Episodes of blackouts, dizziness, fainting, nausea, blurred vision, auras, etc. (cf. Item 5).
7. Sensory impairments.
8. Acute or chronic bleeding from sense organs.
9. Addictions or habituations (barbituates, narcotics, alcohol, etc.).
10. Familial mental illness (specify).
11. Allergies.
12. Prolonged bed-wetting or constipation.

Current Status

1. General physical appearance (body size, obvious state of health, etc.).
2. Obvious scars, marks, or other physical defects.
3. Level of ambulation (walking, wheelchair, etc.).
4. Posture, gait, coordination.
5. Presence of glasses, hearing aid, or orthopedic appliances
6. Neatness and appearance of clothing.
7. Care of hair, finger nails, and teeth.
8. Obvious body odors (due to hygenic or organic factors)
9. Speech impairments (type).
10. Overt restlessness, or lack of.
11. Physical ailments or complaints.
12. Recent loss or gain of weight.
13. Appetite.
14. Sleep habits.
15. Presence of incontinence.
16. Acute physical illness during interview (heart attack, appendicitis, etc.).

Mental Status

This is the crux of the psychiatric examination. The cognitive, intellectual, emotional, and behavioral spheres are examined as crucial factors in a client's mental status and are the following.

Cognitive Factors

1. State of awareness (clear, clouded, stuporous, delirious, comatose, etc.).
2. Perceptual responses in general.

3. Memory for recent and past events.
4. Degree of orientation to time, place, and person.
5. Ideation (flight of ideas, bizarreness, etc.).
6. Attention span and level of concentration.
7. Hallucinations, type and content.
8. Delusions, type and content.
9. Level of insight.
10. Level of judgment.

Intellectual Factors (in lieu of psychometrics)

1. Over-all mental alertness.
2. Attention span and level of concentration.
3. Quantity and quality of verbal responses.
4. Age-education-knowledge ratios.
5. Molecular or field approach to intellectual tasks.
6. Ability to understand environment.
7. Problem-solving ability, concrete and abstract.
8. Ability and willingness to work or think spontaneously.
9. Ability and willingness to finish an intellectual task.

Emotional Factors

1. Appropriateness and type of emotionality or mood (affect).
2. Distractiveness, flight of ideas, or confusion.
3. Degree and level of orientation to reality.
4. Negativism, rigidity, or blocking.
5. Thought content (ideation).
6. Fantasy processes (day or night dreams, hallucinations, delusions, etc.).
7. Suicidal or homicidal preoccuptions.
8. Psychosomatic manifestations (ulcers, palpitations, migraine, skin rashes, hyperventilation, etc.).
9. Presence of and degree of depression.
10. Hostile and aggressive features.
11. Blaming or condemning attitude.
12. Authoritarian feelings (rigidity, power aspirations, stereotypy, etc.).
13. Positivism, flexibility, freedom of expression.
14. Level of spontaneity.
15. Friendly, shy, or autistic emotionality.
16. Presence of humor.
17. Problem area (sexual, religious, marital, employment, etc.).
18. Attitude toward proposed treatment.
19. Motivation for behavioral and emotional change.

Behavioral Factors

1. Affective behavior or mood (bland, flat, spontaneous, manic, autistic, etc.).
2. Presence of habit mechanisms (tics, nailbiting, smoking, etc.).
3. Overt emotions (tears, blushing, fear, shaking, anger, etc.).
4. Reaction to any specific stimulus objects or situations in or outside of the examining room.
5. Compulsive behavior (rocking, pacing, scratching, etc.).
6. Daydreaming of an obvious nature.
7. Catatonic behavior (mutism, negativism, stupor, rigid posture, etc.).
8. Psychosomatic manifestations (acute skin rash, etc.).
9. Verbalized hallucinatory material.
10. Task approach to verbal and performance evaluative measures (counting, recitation, etc.).
11. Sexual manifestations (exhibitionism, masturbation, advances toward clinician, etc.).
12. Threats to clinician (verbal or physical).
13. Adaptive behavior (fainting, nausea, toilet emergency, etc.).
14. Acute physical illness.

Social Behavior

Social interactions in general should be considered, both pretreatment and at the time of hospitalization. Some of this material may inadvertently overlap with that contained in the developmental history. These areas are the following:

Pretreatment

1. Family and peer-group relations.
2. School social behavior.
3. Pattern and type of any antisocial behavior.
4. Criminal actions and convictions, if any.
5. Manner in which anxiety and frustration are handled (internalized or acted-out).
6. Tendency to be an isolate or a joiner.
7. Employment relations.
8. Leadership qualities.
9. Recreational and leisure-time pursuits.

During Treatment (especially for follow-up reports)

1. Acceptance of hospital or clinic treatment.
2. Quality and quantity of social interactions.

3. Degree of participant-observer interactions.
4. Response to treatment milieu.
5. Modification of pretreatment behavior and ideation.
6. Ability to get along with ward peers, family, friends, and other associates.

As with other procedural outlines presented in this text, this outline should function as a guide by which to conduct a psychiatric examination leading to a report, and a prototype for formulating other diagnostic interview models. If the report writer was to comment on *each* point outlined for every client, then the report would be unnecessarily lengthy in most cases. Still, one may have occasion to comment on many of these points with some clients who display involved cases and histories. At any rate, if the clinician only reports on positive factors (items *present* in a case) and not on nonexistent conditions (negative factors) then the report will probably be more reasonable in length. It would be rather superfluous for a clinician to say, for example, "the client had the usual childhood diseases, but *no* previous serious illnesses, dizziness, blackouts, epilepsy, and alcoholism were evident." Here, the statement, "the client had the usual childhood diseases," would be adequate with no additional comments being made in this area, unless specifically justified in a given situation. The reader should consult a text on the dynamics of interviewing if he feels especially deficient in this area.

THE ACTUAL REPORT

When in final form most reports will reflect a certain individualized quality as directed by the writer, his employing organization, and the needs of the future readers. Resultantly, reports prepared by a high school counselor may be quite different in scope than that of the person doing rehabilitation counseling. Both may be different from those written by the physician or the clinical psychologist. Social workers may write still different styles of reports. Several reports will be illustrated next as taken from actual clinical cases among several hospitals and counseling centers. These reports, as well as others throughout the book will, on occasion, use a fictitious or hypothetical report in order to illustrate a given report situation.

Psychiatric Examination

Case No. 3   July 6, 19_____

This twenty-seven-year-old white single male was admitted to _________________ Hospital on July 6, 19_____, under order of a physician's certificate. It was reported by the referring physician that the patient was irrational, hyperactive, and aggressive, thereby creating a hazard to the well-being of others around him.

The patient has a B.S. degree in Sociology. His medical record indicates a suicide attempt eight years ago (an overdose of barbituates was taken) during an episode of acute depression. As a result, he was hospitalized for several days and then sent back to school. Five years ago, he was admitted to _________________ Hospital where he remained for two years and was then given a discharge. One year later he returned to this same hospital and was diagnosed as, "schizophrenic reaction, catatonic type." At that time he was receiving an extremely large dosage, in excess of _____ mg per day, of a tranquilizing drug. Antidepressants were simultaneously being given. He was discharged after a few months.

This patient was admitted to _________________ Hospital on July 6, 19_____; he was seen for a psychiatric examination. Today, on interview, he appeared restless, agitated, talked incessantly, showed tangentiality, and blocked on certain questions. He seemed to be free of any delusional or hallucinatory experiences at this time. His affect was flat. His mood was depressed and his insight and judgment were poor. He was oriented as to time, place, and person; however, his intellectual knowledge of his environment seemed to be within average limits.

Diagnostic Impression
Schizophrenic reaction, chronic undifferentiated type, with depressive features.

Prognosis
Uncertain at this time.

Conditions for Release
Relief of present symptomology.

Recommendations
Phenothiazinic drugs (specified). Group psychotherapy and industrial-occupational remotivation and practical work assignments.

(Signed) John Doe, M.D.
Staff Psychiatrist

Psychiatric Examination

Case No. 4   June 28, 19______

This thirty-three-year-old white married female was admitted to ___________________ Hospital two weeks ago on an involuntary basis. On admission she was anxious, suspicious, and somewhat incoherent. She is a housewife and has a high school education.

Historically, this patient had been hospitalized twice before at her husband's request. On these two occasions she displayed strong feelings of suspiciousness, ideas of reference, and delusions of persecution.

Mental status examination today revealed a woman who denied any delusions or hallucinations. She was very guarded in her responses and attempted to convince the interviewer that she was not mentally ill, and that family difficulties were her greatest problem. The patient was oriented as to time, place, and person, and her memory for recent and past events was good. Good judgment was indicated but her insight was below average.

Diagnostic Impression

Schizophrenic reaction, paranoid type in remission.

Prognosis

Good with resolution of family problems; however, her long-term prognosis is uncertain.

Recommendations

Phenothiazinic drugs (specified), daily. The patient should participate in occupational, recreational, and group psychotherapy meetings. Prior to discharge this patient should undergo marriage and family counseling with her husband. Post-discharge psychotherapy and chemotherapy seem probable.

(Signed) John Doe, M.D.
Staff Psychiatrist

The reader will have probably already concluded that the psychiatric examination reports presented on Case No. 3 and Case No. 4 did not include very much of the report criteria outlined earlier in this chapter. How true! These two reports told some of the facts but many were omitted that could have been obtained from the patient in most instances. Additionally, the vocabulary used in these reports was somewhat discipline specific. The report on Case No. 5 will illustrate how this can happen through no fault of the interviewer.

Psychiatric Examination

Case No. 5   April 12, 19______

This twenty-three-year-old white single female was admitted to ________________ Hospital from the ________________ County Jail. She was accompanied to the hospital by the ________________ County Police.

The patient appeared as a well-nourished female who refused to speak to the interviewer (the police reported that she spoke only a little to them). She wore glasses, and was dressed in a pair of dirty blue jeans and a blouse. Her hair was unkempt and her general appearance was very dirty.

She reacted to mechanically induced auditory stimuli which indicated that there was no functional or organic hearing impairment.

The police related that the patient had been picked up in a bar where she had been attempting to purchase marijuana. While en route to the jail she had leaped from the police car at a stop sign and had fallen into a ditch. After being booked on a narcotics charge the patient became quite erratic in her behavior—she cursed the officers severely, made numerous hostile verbal and physical threats toward them, and was generally unmanageable. She was then brought to the ________________ Hospital on an emergency admission status, after which she refused to speak to anyone.

Diagnostic Impression
Drug dependence reaction, cannabis sativa, with psychotic reaction.

Prognosis
Guarded.

Precautions
Possible elopement.

Recommendations
Complete psychological evaluation, after which plan treatment program in detail.

(Signed) Mary Doe, M.A.
Psychologist

The patient in Case No. 5 could not be questioned in the routine manner due to her refusal to converse with the interviewer. Therefore, it was necessary to question a third party (the police in this case) in order to obtain any details pertaining to her case.

The next psychiatric examination report is a good example of a more comprehensive interview on which to base the report. It should be noted that even this report does not encompass *all* of the points present in the earlier outline. However, the significant points as related to this case seem to have been brought out.

Psychiatric Examination

Case No. 6   August 1, 19____

This thirty-year-old white single male admitted himself voluntarily at the request of his family to the ________________ Mental Health Clinic three days ago, on July 29, 19____. He was accompanied to the Clinic by his father.

When the patient was admitted he was very unkempt in dress, dirty, as well as being in need of a shave and a haircut. At the time of his admission he had been living in a barn outside of the city limits of ________________ in ________________ county.

Historically, the patient has a ninth-grade education (he quit school) and is of the protestant religion. He has two older brothers (apparently well adjusted) who are married and living away from their parent's home. The only problems of a medical nature the patient seems to have had were the usual childhood diseases. His mother passed away four years ago, in 19____. Throughout his school years (and after) he was a loner and did not interact well with his peers or teachers. Seven years ago, in 19____, he admitted himself to the ________________ State Hospital on two separate occasions; on the last, he was hospitalized for approximately three months. He had obtained a WB-I IQ of 94 during that last hospital stay. After leaving the psychiatric facility, he spent approximately three weeks at a medical-surgical hospital where he received a series of electroshock treatments (quantity unknown). A year ago, in 19____, he had one other admission to the ________________ State Hospital: he had been picked up by the police for possessing a pistol on his person. A week before this present admission he had spent four days in jail on a vagrancy charge.

Mental status examination revealed on this present admission that the patient is a rather belligerent and anxious man who tends to withdraw from others. He stated that as long as he could remember that he didn't like to be around other people and preferred to be alone. His gait was very determined, as he took large definite steps. The patient giggled inappropriately when asked questions by the interviewer. His speech was soft, muddled, and at times incoherent. When asked to speak louder, he would burst out in a loud voice in a seemingly hostile manner. The patient related that on one or more occasions he had "beaten up his sister-in-law" for reasons which he would not reveal. There was no other admission of physical aggression toward others on the part of the patient. He further said that he preferred to be alone and "didn't want any part of other people as they would cause you trouble." He had been unsuccessful at even holding down a job and "didn't see any point in working."

This man is oriented as to time, place, and person; and any delusional or hallucinatory experiences were denied. When he was asked specific questions of why he felt the way he did, he said, "it ain't none of your business." He did mention, however, that he could "get back at others who bothered him" if he felt he wanted to do so. Additionally, he mentioned that he would leave the hospital if he had a chance, with or without a discharge. He appears to be within average intellectual limits.

Diagnostic Impression
Schizophrenic reaction, chronic undifferentiated type, with strong passive-aggressive features.

Prognosis
Poor, due to his unwillingness to accept treatment.

Precautions
Elopement and physical assault.

Recommendations
Transfer to and confinement in a State Hospital for ninety days to provide intensive, reality-oriented psychotherapy. Remotivation therapy. Recreational therapy. Reevaluation in ninety days.

(Signed) Mary Doe, M.A.
Psychologist

The psychiatric examination on the patient in Case No. 6 was more comprehensive than those in the other sample reports. The latter report was arbitrarily divided into four sections. This format is a rather easy one to follow as the report writer does not have to decide on several subdivisions of the report, since a number of items were overlapped within these four categories.

The reader will recall that in Chapter III, sixteen report topic areas were outlined. However, for practical purposes the actual report is not usually divided into so many sections in the final typed form. The only "test" administered in a psychiatric examination per se is the interview. Similarly, the other categories which were outlined are combined, and at times altered, thereby conforming to a report format which is informative and easily read.

Chapter IX

THE INTELLECTUAL EVALUATION

THE PSYCHOLOGIST or counselor will at times be asked to conduct a specific type of examination on his client. Where the social history statement was essentially a part of any examination, and the psychiatric examination is usually thought of as being an evaluation resulting from an interview, the *intellectual evaluation* is obtained more frequently from test data. The reader will recall that an estimate of the client's intellectual capacity can be obtained during the course of the psychiatric examination. However, a more concrete type of an evaluation would come from the administration of standardized psychological tests.

There are any number of good tests on the market for obtaining an index of the client's intellectual functioning. Traditionally, the Wechsler and the Binet scales have been the standard bearers of both children's and adult's intellectual assessment. The reader is undoubtedly aware that there are several other tests available as well as different ways in which to measure and view intelligence. And, the question of "what *is* intelligence?" has been defined in any number of ways by as many different writers.

THE IMPORTANCE OF INTELLECTUAL DATA

Since a client's intellectual capacity is only a part of his global environmental functioning, knowledge of his measured intelligence is important in the psychological evaluation. The level of any person's intelligence will determine in many ways how he views and subsequently interacts with his environment. The mentally retarded individual will have a different perception and response mode than will the average or the gifted person. The level of one's intelligence will also have a strong bearing upon his achievement in academic areas as well as upon his success in the occupational areas. Therefore, through the administration of tests of intelligence the clinician will be in a much better position to prepare a report of his client's intellectual status, thereby complementing the therapeutic modalities.

In the school setting the counselor may wish to obtain the student's intelligence quotients to aid placement decisions in special classes or for advising them about special curriculums. Without knowledge of intellectual functioning, some exceptional students could be misplaced in their academic courses as well as subjected to course material below or above their ability level. In the psychiatric setting certain types of treatment may very well be contingent upon the patient's intellectual ability. Knowledge of the client's intellectual functioning can lend support to the planning of treatment programs in the areas of academic, social, vocational, and the many areas of personal counseling.

INDIVIDUAL OR GROUP TESTS?

The clinician will be the best judge of which test of intelligence and its form to use. And, this decision may best be made in terms of the purposes of the testing. Mass screening examinations may be better suited for testing students in the school setting while individualized tests may be best for the referral cases.

In some situations a rapid measure of intelligence may be all that is necessary in order to supplement a client's record or to serve as a screening device. On the other hand, if both general and specific factors of intelligence are needed, then one of the individually administered tests would be more appropriate.

The intellectual evaluation may appear as a single report or as a portion of the comprehensive psychological evaluation. In either case, a standardized test should be administered. If for some reason a test cannot be given, then the clinician must rely upon data from the interview in order to obtain an *estimate* of the client's intellectual level.

THE ACTUAL REPORT

After either the psychologist or the counselor has administered one or more intelligence tests to a client, and the tests have been scored and interpreted, then the report on the intellectual evaluation will be made. This report, like any other special purpose report, will have certain commonalities of structure. Also, since certain behavioral, personality, and organic findings may be inferred from the intelligence test data, these findings are usually reported.

The following report on Case No. 7 was based on the administration of a single intelligence test.

Psychological Report

Case No. 7   Date________________

Client: (Name)

Test Administered
Wechsler Adult Intelligence Scale (WAIS)

This single white male, aged nineteen, was seen for an intellectual evaluation on ____________, 19____. He is a freshman college student and has not chosen a major field of study. He referred himself.

He was very receptive to the testing session and did not seem to manifest any overt anxiety or apprehension. He was neatly dressed and his personal appearance was good. His speech was normal as to tone, diction, and rate. He seemed to be oriented as to time, place, and person.

Intellectual Findings
He received a Verbal IQ of 100, a Performance IQ of 116, and a Full Scale IQ of 107 on the *WAIS*. His verbal level was 16 points below his performance level and this seemed to be due, in part, to impoverishment of responses on the Information, Arithmetic, Similarities, and the Digit Span subtests. The lower Verbal IQ also suggests a personality malfunction of a sociopathic nature.

Intratest and intertest variability were pronounced on most subtests; and, some easy items were missed. On the Similarities subtest the examinee repeated the paired words as "answers" and gave the reply, "they are opposites" on other paired words. In general, his answers were above average in concretism. On Arithmetic and Digit Span low scaled scores were obtained while high-scaled scores were made on Block Design and Object Assembly. This combination seemed to indicate, in part, a discrepancy in his ability to execute tasks on effort. Also, the low scores are suggestive of anxiety and possible organicity while his high scores on the performance measures tend to rule out the organic indications.

For the most part, he tended to give up easily on the verbal sub-tests while much enthusiasm was shown for the performance sub-tests. Another significant point is that he seemed to be more concerned with impressing the examiner with his speed of task execution than with being accurate in his answers.

Diagnosis

Average Intelligence with possible Personality Disorder.

Recommendations

A personality evaluation should be conducted on this client, after which, a personality diagnosis and treatment recommendations (if any) should be made.

(Signed) John Doe, M.S.
Psychologist

The student in Case No. 7 seemed to manifest several suspicious personality responses on the intelligence test. Therefore, a follow-up personality evaluation was recommended. Since he was of average intelligence, no recommendations were felt to be necessary from this standpoint. However, the psychologist could very well have recommended aptitude or achievement tests in order to better ascertain his level of functioning at the college level.

Case No. 8 illustrates a situation where the student's teacher and principal requested an intellectual evaluation in order to better plan his course work. Mental retardation was suspected and this was the major reason for this examination having been requested.

Psychological Report

Case No. 8   Date________________

Client: (Name)

Age: 9-9   Grade: Second

A diagnostic evaluation on this second grade male student was requested by his teacher and principal. The testing was conducted on ________________, 19______, at the Midtown Psychological Clinic. The purpose of the examination was to ascertain the intellectual level of this client.

Tests Administered

Wechsler Intelligence Scale for Children (WISC), *Ammons Full-Range Picture Vocabulary Test* (FRPV), and *Goodenough Draw-A-Man Test* (DAM).

General Observations

This student was very cooperative during the testing session and sat quietly during the entire battery of tests. Very few words were spoken by him. He smiled frequently and seemed to enjoy the tests, except the ones which called for verbal responses. He seemed to be very shy, and aloof toward the examiner. Physically, he was very clean in appearance. He seemed to be about twenty to thirty pounds underweight for his stature and age.

Psychometric Results

WISC	Verbal IQ	48
	Performance IQ	76
	Full Scale IQ	58
FRPV	Verbal IQ	67
	Mental Age (years)	6.8
DAM	Estimated IQ	82
	Mental Age (years)	8.0

Inasmuch as this student was not willing to give many verbal responses it is felt that his verbal scores underestimate his true ability. Therefore, his performance scores should be considered as more indicative of his maximum intellectual level.

The three tests yielded significantly different intelligence quotients, but the scores were close enough to obtain an estimate of his ability. The content of his verbal responses (taking into consideration the limited number given) were very concretistic and impoverished, which seemed to indicate poor responses to the academic situation—some of this may have been due to poor preschool readiness training, as many easy items were missed. The Verbal IQ of 48 on the *WISC* does not seem to reflect his true ability; the Verbal IQ of 67 on the *FRPV* test is probably more realistic of his verbal ability in terms of word comprehension and understanding. The much higher performance ability which indicated a Performance IQ of 76 on the *WISC* and an estimated IQ of 82 on the *DAM* test probably reflect the maximum ability of this student.

Diagnosis

Mental retardation, moderate.

Recommendations

This student should be referred to a special education unit for individualized instruction. Verbal and social interaction skills should be emphasized.

His over-all curriculum should be directed toward vocational rather than academic areas, due to his severe language skill impairment and borderline intelligence. The areas of pursuit might be those related to industrial arts and crafts such as carpentry, mechanics, or any similar types of skilled labor. Apprenticeship training would seem to be effective.

Curriculum planning should be directed toward providing this student with an opportunity to realize personal achievement and competency in his own way. He should learn to take pride in his work and to receive personal, intrinsic satisfaction for his efforts.

(Signed) John Doe, M.S.
Psychologist

With Case No. 8, a somewhat different format was used for the report. First, the date and purpose of the examination along with other identifying data were presented in the first part of the report. The second paragraph was used to list the three intelligence tests which were administered. A special section, "Psychometric Results," was used to list the results of the three tests. Next, a rather lengthy recommendations section was incorporated. These recommendations provided specifics for the teacher to consider using in planning this student's curriculum.

The next psychological report is of a special type. In this report on Case No. 9, only one test, the *Goodenough Draw-A-Man*, was administered. This ten-year-old student had been previously tested and the *Draw-A-Man* test was used as an interim evaluation instrument.

Psychological Report

Case No. 9   Date_______________

Client: (Name)
Age: 10-10   Grade: Fourth
Referred by: Miss Jones, fourth grade teacher.

This white, fourth grade student was referred by Miss Jones for an interim diagnostic intellectual evaluation. He was seen by the elementary counselor on _________________, 19____.

Presenting Problem

The student's teacher reported that he was having marked difficulty in classroom work of the fourth grade level. It was also reported that a previous psychological examination had been conducted six months ago. At that time he obtained an IQ of 87. Additionally, the student's parents had been advised that he be placed in a special class for slow learners; however, his parents strongly refused to allow this transfer. The teacher reported that this student was liked a great deal by his peers and that he "always displays a happy, cooperative manner at school." He seems to try his best in his school work.

Intellectual Findings

This student was administered one test, the *Goodenough Draw-A-Man* (DAM). On the test he made a raw score of 10 which indicated a mental age of 5-6, thereby placing him at the educably mentally retarded level, at the very most. This IQ of 51 in conjunction with a previous IQ of 87 appears to indicate the range of his intellectual functioning. On the *DAM* test he definitely functioned as a retarded child as his reproductions were of a primitive nature (stick man with little detail) as well as having poor psychomotor coordination in the lines.

Sociopersonal Findings

In conjunction with the *DAM* test, a "draw your family" exercise was undertaken by the student. These results indicated that the father was drawn quite large thereby indicating his being a dominant and looked-up-to figure in the family structure. The mother figure was drawn in the background which tended to place her as a passive member of the family. He drew himself as an unimportant member of the family; this was shown by a miniaturization of his own figure. All family members were depicted as smiling which seemed to indicate the presence of a cohesive family structure.

Diagnostic Impression

Mental retardation, mild.

Recommendations

Conduct a comprehensive psychological evaluation including one or more individual tests of intelligence and personality. Also, one or two measures of organicity should be administered.

Plan this student's placement and curriculum on the basis of the findings from the comprehensive psychological evaluation.

(Signed) John Doe, M.Ed.
Counselor

The evaluation on the student presented in Case No. 9 was used primarily for a point of illustration: that one *cannot* conduct an *adequate* intellectual or personality evaluation on the basis of a drawing alone. Few, if any, school systems (or States) will accept the results of a test of this type for classification as "mentally retarded" for subsequent placement in either a special education unit or a State school for the retarded. Usually, one must administer at least one (and sometimes two) standardized, individual tests of intelligence such as the Wechsler or Binet scales. Another point in regard to this particular report is that a single report would not usually be prepared on a "drawing analysis" as the psychologist or counselor would probably proceed with the administration of other tests of intelligence and then prepare a full report. Minimally, this procedure would eliminate the need for writing two separate reports.

As mentioned previously, a psychological report on *only* intellectual material per se is a rare bird, as is a report on solely personality or organic findings. The clinician usually includes the "facts" of a given special report, and then infers subjective data on other areas of functioning by observing the client. Also, one may infer emotional and organic parameters of intelligence from a given comprehensive intelligence test.

At times, an intellectual evaluation may be used for classroom grouping, or special student placement. It may also be used for screening in psychotherapy groups. An additional function of an intellectual evaluation is to provide a reference point for aptitude and achievement test results in order to ascertain whether or not a student or client is achieving with, above, or below his level or the group norm. A multifactor test of intelligence may also yield significant data on special abilities or deficits of the client; and, the psychologist or counselor can use this information as a baseline for other supportive, specialized psychometric measures.

Chapter X

THE PERSONALITY EVALUATION

EVEN THOUGH a formalized personality evaluation has similar content to that of a psychiatric examination, the latter is based on an interview with the patient or client. Psychological tests or rating scales are used to supply the clinician with the necessary data for preparing the *personality evaluation* report. Media which are self-report, rater-ratee, or clinician administered will supply both subjective and objective information on one's client. At times, an interview may precede the actual testing activities with one's notes being included in the final report. However, if a report is titled a "Personality Evaluation" or states this specifically in the report body, then neither organic, intellectual, nor other test results should be included.

Any report designated as an intellectual, personality, or organic evaluation alone will not be as ultimately useful as a more comprehensive one. An occasion may very well arise, however, for one to prepare one of these single purpose reports.

The first sample report, Case No. 10, includes the data from only one personality test. In this particular report, the writer included a transcribed protocol of the client's responses which were taken from a mechanical tape recording. In this procedure, the clinician presents the actual "facts" (verbatim recording) and then makes an interpretation.

Personality Evaluation

Case No. 10   Date________________

Client: (Name)
Referred by: Self
Test Administered
   Make A Picture Story (MAPS)

This twenty-six-year-old white single male voluntarily sought treatment at the University Counseling Center. His classification is a junior. He was seen on ________________, 19____, for a personality evaluation.

Presenting Problem

This student reported that he was having difficulty in his college courses. Also, he said, "I have been feeling sad, tired, and having difficulty in my relations with girls." He further mentioned that his parents were divorced and that he was an only child. Other than his having diabetes mellitus, he appears to be in good physical condition.

The MAPS Protocol

The client was administered eight *MAPS* scenes. The transcript of the taped dialogue for each of these scenes is as follows:

Living Room

Client: Ah—in this sequence the father [M-10] has just come home from town; he's carrying gifts under his arm, and apparently he has just opened the door and called to his family. Ah—there are three other figures in the sequence—ah—a mother [N-6], a little girl [C-2], and a little boy [C-7]. And, the little boy seems quite anxious to see what his father has for him. The little girl is not so anxious; she has her back turned to him and she's got a pouting expression on her face, and this is probably because she was quite severely scolded by her father earlier in the day. The mother is to the extreme left of the scene; she is attempting to—uh—make her daughter come out of this—uh—pouting in this situation she is in. That should conclude the story.

Therapist: Ok. That was good. Let's try this next one.

Cl. All right.

Street

Cl. Umm hmm. Ok. In this sequence we have a rather serious human drama [sighs and catches his breath], guess you might say. A scene is downtown in a rather slummy part of town you might say [long pause]. There are four figures in the sequence. Ah—a—man injured or a dead man [M-7] lies on the sidewalk, and two women [F-5] and [F-7] and a man [M-6] with a gun. Ah—the man with a gun has just shot this other man lying on the ground and two women are standing by in—ah—showing signs of extreme horror, fear. The—ah—man has shot this other man because—uh—he's been trifling with his wife. And—out in the hope he has, in a fit of rage, shot this other man and this is the end of the sequence.

Th. Ok. You have any specific names for any of the people?
Cl. No.
Th. Try this one now.

Medical

Cl. This one takes place in the doctor's office—ah—there are three figures—nude woman [F-1], a sick man [I-1], and a doctor [M-9]. Apparently this doctor is a very busy man and may have more business than he can take care of. He's got this woman—uh—this nude woman—uh—scheduled for a physical examination, but at the same time he's also got a sick man, apparently unconscious, uh—lying on—uh—the examination table. And it appears that he's just come in from making a house call, so this is—uh—three things that he's had to take care of just within perhaps an hour's time—half an hour's time. Ok, that should conclude that story.
Th. Ok. Now let's try this one.

Bathroom

Cl. Uh—little shorter this time. The sequence is that of two characters in the bathroom scene—uh—uh—a naked boy [C-6],—uh—a dressed woman [F-4]. Uh—the scene the woman has just drawn a bath for the boy and—uh—he's come into the bathroom to get ready to take a bath; and, she has her back turned, and she says—uh—for the sake of modesty, she says, 'ok, son—uh—I'll turn my back while you get into the tub.' And that's the end of the sequence.
Th. About how old is the boy?
Cl. Mmmmm—I'd say about nine or ten.
Th. Ok. Let's try the next one.

Dream

Cl. In this sequence we have—uh—four characters—a—uh—three of the characters are within the thoughts of one character [the dreamer]. And—this—uh—man who presumably is doing the thinking is uh—perhaps asleep, dreaming this situation. And uh, there are, the other three characters in the drama are—uh—[long pause]—they are—a semi-nude woman [F-2] and a man [M-2] and the third figure [M-12], which is a man listening, or looking through a keyhole. Ah—the—uh—sequence of events that's taking place, this uh—first figure is dreaming [background image] —uh —this man who is undressing is having, or about to have sexual relations with his the other man's wife. And, uh, he appears himself [the dreamer] as the man listening [M-12], at the wall or at the door; and, he has just come on the scene where the—uh—events are going on in that room. He says, 'Uh-hmmm, they're at it again —I'll catch em this time—just let me listen to em for awhile and when they're right in the middle of the act I'll burst in on em and surprise them.' And, this is because this man has—uh—this uh— doing the uh—dreaming, the listening, has long suspected his wife of having sexual relations with another man. And, this dream, he uh—believes that he will uh—that he has wanted to think about for a long time—wanted to be able to do this to catch this man and his [dreamer, M-12] wife together. And, this is the end of this sequence.

Th. So the man who is dreaming is the same one that is listening.
Cl. Ummm-hmmm. Yes.
Th. Let's try this bridge scene next.

Bridge
Cl. In this sequence we have five actors or whatever you want to call them in the drama. There is a policeman [M-4], a soldier [M-3], a businessman [M-13], and a rather poorly dressed woman [F-4]. The scene takes place on a bridge, over a river in a large city, in the United States. Ah—[coughs], there's a man [S-1] whose silhouette is only visible; he's standing up on the edge of the bridge, prepared to jump and the soldier, and businessman, and poorly dressed woman are bystanders—uh—looking on at this situation that's about to happen. The policeman has just come up and sternly orders the man, about to commit suicide, to get down off the bridge at once. This is the conclusion of the—drama.

Th. Are any of these people related to one another?
Cl. No.
Th. No specific identity.
Cl. No.
Th. Here is the next one.

Bedroom
Cl. In this scene—uh—bedroom layout and uh, there is a man [M-2] and a woman [F-2]; they're undressed, preparing to go to bed. Ah—they're not married to each other, in fact—uh—the uh— woman's husband [S-1] is standing outside the window; he suspects a situation of them—uh—having goings on with each other; and, this—this is a shadow [S-1] figure—uh—outside of the window; even though the uh—figure [S-1] seems to be within the room. Ah —and—this uh—people are more or less in double jeopardy because —ah, they don't know that there is another figure lying in the bed there. They think that the bedroom is empty; but there is another figure and this is well enough disguised to where they don't think

there is anyone in the room but themselves. And, this is the end of this sequence.

Th. Is this figure [background] that's lying in the bed, male or female?

Cl. This is the uh—this is the wife of the man that is getting undressed.

Th. And the silhouette is the husband of the woman?

Cl. Yes.

Th. This next one is a little different. You are to imagine a scene on this blank background and then place your figures as you have done so in each of the other backgrounds. You may begin.

Blank

Cl. Uh—this scene—uh—is the background in a—Harlem section of one of the cities; and uh—in it we have uh—four Negro figures, and two white figures. Ah—there are two old Negroes [N-1 and N-2] and two fairly young ones [N-5 and N-9]—uh—there is an— old Negro man and an old Negro woman together. And—in front of them is a young Negro man [N-5] and a young Negro woman [N-9]. The uh—young Negro man is carrying a knife which he apparently—uh—or rather a razor blade or something to this effect —straight razor—uh—which he's apparently getting ready to use on somebody; and, he's carrying a chain, hanging off his belt. I presume it is hanging out from under his coat. Ah—he appears to be a street fighter type of person; and, the Negro woman behind him is uh—seems like the tough—street—woman of the streets type of woman. There's a very short skirt and a turtle-neck type sweater [on the young Negro woman]—and, the uh—two white figures [M-6 and F-8] consist of uh—uh—uh—a white woman— who is apparently quite angered or upset and behind her is uh— a balding white man who is carrying a gun. And, what has happened is that—uh these white people, neither one them like Negroes, but uh—through some circumstance they've found them- selves in a Negro neighborhood—and—the—white man has insulted the old Negro man and old Negro woman, and the young Negro man is coming to their rescue to uh—uh—more or less avenge the insult of the white man, and seems to be quite well prepared and carried an automatic pistol with him—and which he is pointing at the Negro man [N-5] with the razor blade; and, the white woman is shouting more insults at the Negroes. That's the end of this sequence.

Th. Is the old couple related to the young couple?

Cl. Ah—yes—the uh—the uh—Negro man [N-5] is their [N-1 and N-2] son. The Negro woman [N-9] has no relation—she is uh—the Negro man's [N-5] uh—uh—long pause—fiance or whatever you want to call her.

Th. And, what about the white couple?

Cl. Well, they're married to each other.

Analysis of the Protocol

Analysis of the *MAPS* transcript indicated a high level of interaction among the figures. There was the presence of open sexuality in four out of eight scenes. Self-referral was especially noted in the *Dream* scene. Direct evidence of violence was shown in both the *Street* and the *Blank* scenes. Evidence of violence was also present in the *Medical* scene along with overt sexuality being indicated. New figures were chosen in each scene except figures M-6, M-2, F-2, and S-1: these four figures were chosen twice each. All figures were correctly oriented as to space except S-1 which was depicted as being suspended.

Suicidal fantasies were shown in the *Bridge* scene. Interpersonal relations were happy in the *Living Room* scene—interestingly enough, there was a Negro mother and a white father and child present. The *Bathroom* scene indicated an attempt to cover up overt sexuality through a facade of sexual modesty on the part of the two figures: this was a sharp contrast to the other themes of sexual starkness. In the *Dream*, *Bridge*, and *Bedroom* scenes there was a great deal of self-reference in that the silhouette was used twice and the dreamer's self was used. The females in each of the scenes were depicted in most instances as being shocked, surprised, or in fear; Negro women were used three times and two of the women appeared to be from the lower social class. One Negro woman was of the southern "mammy" type. Except in sexual and family scenes, all men were involved in a violent situation of one type or another. The children in the scenes were shown as being both demanding and dependent upon their parents.

The verbatim protocol indicated emotional blocking or resistance in nearly each scene where female figures were involved. This is indicated by numerous pauses, hesitations, and the like. This may be representative of repressed conflicts over sexual roles and activities. In scenes displaying a basically violent content, little blocking was noted. Generally, there was a great deal of fantasizing activity as well as a tendency to create stories with abundant suspicious, mistrusting, and bizarre themes. The client seemed to have difficulty in facing sexual situations for what they were, as he had a tendency to be overly modest in his choice of words in scenes evidencing sexual content. Furthermore, the client tended to over-elaborate his responses and gave a great deal of attention to minor details. His ability to synthesize parts into global situations is complementary to his high IQ of 126.

In summary, the client displayed what seems to be a marked conflict over sexual matters, especially in relation to heterosexual activities. There was considerable hostility toward females; and, a great deal of hostility was shown toward male authority figures and minority groups. Depressive signs were above average. The possibility of one or more childhood traumas in regard to sexual activities of his parents seems to be indicated. Interpersonal relationships seem to be difficult for this client to handle with any degree of effectiveness.

Diagnosis

Personality pattern disturbance, schizoid type, with reactive depression, moderate.

Prognosis

Good for the depression; guarded for the pre-psychotic thinking.

Recommendations

Begin intensive individual psychotherapy three times weekly for a minimum of twelve weeks. The client should be reevaluated at the end of the thirty-six sessions. The psychotherapy sessions should be directed toward elevating this client's self-concept and problem-solving skills in the social setting. Assist the client in establishing future employment and academic goals. A complete physical examination should be conducted on this client as well as the consideration of psychotropic drugs to treat his depressive symptomology.

(Signed) Mary Doe, M.A.
Psychologist

The psychological report presented on Case No. 10 illustrates a special format. This format concerns the inclusion of *verbatim, transcribed dialogue* between the client and therapist during a projective test session. The use of dialogue vividly describes the client's thinking and feeling tones—this could not have been done with equal success with the use of the therapist's interpretations alone. Of course, this approach produces a very lengthy report; however, when using a projective test this seems to more than offset the disadvantages. One alternative to using the verbatim material in the actual report to be submitted to the reader is to file the transcribed protocol in the case or medical record folder for reference and only include the interpretative comments in the actual report.

The next report, Case No. 11, was sent to the referring physician, and used the results of two personality tests. Also, since there was a medical history of birth injury which may have influenced this client's emotionality, the medical findings were incorporated into the body of the report.

Personality Evaluation

Case No. 11   Date________________

Client: (Name)

Referred by: John Doe, M.D.

Tests Administered

> *Minnesota Multiphasic Personality Inventory* (MMPI) and *Tennessee Self-Concept Scale* (TSCS).

This client is a white, single male aged twenty-three. He dropped out of high school after completing the eleventh grade. He was referred to the Central Diagnostic Center by his family physician, John Doe, for a personality evaluation. He was seen at the Clinic on ________________, 19____.

The client's medical history reveals a brain injury at birth resulting from an instrument delivery; he additionally suffered a total hearing loss in his left ear, as a complication of the birth injury. Previous examination for intelligence and organicity revealed an IQ of 95, with suspicious signs of intracranial pathology on two tests of organicity.

Psychometric Findings

The present personality evaluation revealed the following. On the *MMPI* the client only received one high score (*hypomania*) with all other scores being average or below average. This finding indicates a tendency to be sociable while on the other hand a certain amount of anxiety, deceitfulness, self-dissatisfaction, and rebelling against authority figures is shown.

A counterphobic or reaction-formation type of adjustment, associated with vivid fears and inhibitions, seems to be occurring in the context of pseudo-independence and self-sufficiency. His low score on the *depression* subscale seems to substantiate the acting out of anxiety as one of his primary mechanisms of defense. Thus, one of his dominant features is an under-control of his feelings which has both positive and negative aspects. On the positive side, he is seen as expressive, ebullient, and outgoing. Negatively, he is aggressive, autocratic, egotistical, impulsive, and exhibitionistic. This combination of feelings tends to lead him toward taking the initiative in social interactions and being persuasive and fluent in speech. However, when his lack of control takes on the negative vector he is given to being exhibitionistic, cynical, sarcastic, and counter-attacking when he becomes frustrated. Also, he is given to manipulating others in an attempt to gain his own ends. Much underlying inadequacy is noted, especially along the lines of insecurity in his masculine role. He attempts to overcompensate for his feelings of inadequacy by excessive interest in weight lifting (per interview) and similar showmanship activities.

On the *TSCS* he displays the pattern of a very self-critical and conflictual individual with a low feeling of self-concept. His ideas about his physical prowess are not in keeping with his overall personality, indicating an overconcern for excellence in physical realms. He displays inconsistencies within his own thinking in all areas. Furthermore, he tends to be rather highly opinionated toward a positivistic type of thinking, rejecting the bad, undesirable, or negative realms of existence. High maladjustment, both psychotic and neurotic in nature, was shown throughout the *TSCS* profile.

Diagnosis

Chronic brain syndrome, brain trauma, with personality disorder, passive-aggressive type.

Prognosis

Fair.

Recommendations

Complete neurological examination to rule out any intracranial pathology of a degenerative nature. Intensive individual or group psychotherapy. Consider chemotherapy to control aggressive behavior. Reevaluate in six months. This client should be seen by either a private psychologist or by a community out-patient clinic. However, if his behavior continues to be unmanageable he should be admitted to an in-patient psychiatric facility for intensive treatment.

(Signed) Mary Doe, Ph.D.
Psychologist

The two sample reports presented in this chapter should give the reader some idea of how a personality evaluation report is made. One report incorporated the use of transcribed, tape recorded material. The other used the results of two objective personality tests. Obviously, there are many other possibilities for reporting. The nature of a given report and the tests administered to the client will, in most cases, govern the specific format and language style to use. When objective personality tests are administered the clinician can write a very effective report without using any verbatim material given by the client. On the other hand, when subjective or projective tests have been administered the use of verbatim material greatly clarifies the report content. Many times the nature of personality data can be lost in the realm of a "test score." Therefore, verbatim and explanatory comments are quite helpful in structuring the report.

Finally, as shown in the report on Case No. 11, the omission of previously-obtained medical information and other test findings would have severely limited the diagnostic and interpretive findings in the report. Even though an evaluation, or the subsequent report, may be designated as a specific type does not necessarily mean that the report writer should ignore any other specifically pertinent facts available on one's client. When a report has been specified as an intellectual, organic, personality, or interest evaluation, for example, this does not mean that *only* that information can be included. What it does mean is that the major portion of the report should be devoted to the inherent nature of that particular report, and that all other materials should be excluded unless otherwise justified.

Chapter XI

THE TREATMENT SUMMARY

A TREATMENT SUMMARY is not a psychological report in the usual sense of the word. In particular, psychological tests have not been administered. Essentially, a *treatment summary* is a recapitulation of the client's sessions with the therapist. This account may be a session by session reporting procedure or an over-all view of a given series of therapy sessions. This type of report has also been called a "Progress Note," a "Theragnostic Report," or a "Therapy Report," to name a few.

A report which describes any form of prior, on-going, or *post-facto* behavior of a client which is associated with a given therapeutic regime comes under the category of the treatment summary. Even though it is primarily focused on treatment, the therapist may wish to include relevant psychological test or medical record data in order to amplify his clinical observations of the client. Occasionally, a treatment summary will serve as a diagnostic medium whereby the therapist will describe the client's pretreatment functioning, and evaluate his responses to treatment; then, the therapist will either concur with or modify an existing diagnosis.

Several cases will be illustrated next in order to show the reader the uses and types of *treatment summaries.*

Therapy Progress Report

Case No. 12   Date_______________

Client: (Name)

Therapy dates covered: _______________ to _______________

This forty-nine-year-old white, married male was admitted to the City Psychiatric Clinic on _______________, 19_____. The current psychotherapy series included twice weekly sessions over the above inclusive dates.

At his first therapy session he appeared very rigid in his thinking and displayed tense psychomotor activity. He related that he had been in psychiatric hospitals four or five times since 19______. This patient related that he has been bothered by "nerve trouble" as well as job dissatisfaction for many years. During the ensuing therapy sessions he said very little and tended to sit passively, ignoring the other group members.

Evaluation

This patient is still quite psychotic and his environmental interactions are minimal from the social standpoint. He appears to be a person with a fairly long history of maladjustment and ineffective behavior. He seems to be caught in a vicious circle of conflict and does not appear to realize why he feels the way he does. Intensive therapeutic intervention is strongly recommended for this man and should be continued. The diagnosis of "Schizophrenic reaction, chronic undifferentiated type," is retained.

> (Signed) Mary Smith, M.A.
> Psychologist

The next report, Case No. 13, was made at the point when the patient began having difficulty outside of the therapy group. She had been hospitalized for several months and had been receiving group psychotherapy for several weeks. This progress report was to reevaluate her treatment programming.

Psychotherapy Progress Report

Case No. 13   Date______________

Client: (Name)

Period Covered: Present Status

This thirty-nine-year-old white, single female was referred for consultation by the Rehabilitation Department on ________________, 19______. She has been enrolled in a patient training program for five weeks of a ten-week block.

On interview she was moderately depressed and anxious. She explained that she tried her best to accept the training but that she didn't like the work she was doing. She said she prefers to work in a nursing area. This patient has also received a total of seven psychotherapy sessions as of ________________, 19______. In view of her medical history and her present emotional status, it is strongly recommended that a) she be reassigned to another work area; b) she remain on her same living arrangement; and c) she make a gradual transition to a less structured environment at a later date.

(Signed) John Smith, M.S.
Psychologist

Case No. 14 illustrates another therapy summary report. In this report a format similar to that of a regular psychological report is followed since there is a change of diagnosis after the patient attended a number of psychotherapy sessions.

Theragnostic Report

Case No. 14   Date________________

Client: (Name)

Period Covered: ________________ to ________________.

A pre-therapy interview on ________________, 19______, with this patient revealed that she was admitted to the ________________ Hospital six months ago under a Court commitment. She is a married white female, aged thirty-seven. She spoke with a heavy accent which made conversation very difficult. Her speech was a monotone; the rate was very fast and the phrasing was unbroken. Her thinking processes seemed quite delusional and centered around ideas of persecution. At the time of her admission to this hospital she was diagnosed as "Schizophrenic reaction, paranoid type."

This patient's mental status during her first group therapy session was that of a very confused person. She was incoherent, overly talkative, displayed flight of ideas, and had much difficulty remaining on a topic of discussion. Her conversation centered around her family situation which was very unpleasing to her—she was having a great deal of trouble with her husband and his parents.

During the last of seven group psychotherapy sessions this patient attended, she was a great deal more coherent than she was two months ago. She was readily conversant and seemed to be able to remain on a given topic of discussion for an appreciable length of time. She seemed to be sincerely concerned with the problems of others in the group, especially those who had marital difficulties.

On ________________, 19______, this patient was discharged from the hospital. At the time of her discharge she felt that her husband did love her after all. She seemed to have some insight into her behavior; yet, there seemed to be a residual of problems. However, her thinking was very much improved with no delusional mechanisms in operation. There was a minimum amount of paranoid thinking at this time.

Diagnosis
Schizophrenic reaction, residual type.

Prognosis
Good for the present; fair for future episodes.

Recommendations
This patient should be followed-up by the Division of Family Services on an out-patient basis. She and her husband should also receive marital counseling on an out-patient basis at least once monthly for a period of six months.

(Signed) Mary Doe, Ph.D.
Psychologist

The last three psychotherapy reports were made either during the course of therapy or at the termination of a series of sessions. The next report is somewhat different than the others.

Case No. 15 is presented as an individual psychotherapy session dialogue, after which a diagnosis is given. This report is different from the psychiatric examination in that it is derived from a nondirective interview rather than a structured "examination." It should be pointed out that a therapy report such as the following transcribed protocol is not the most brief manner in which to report on one's case, as was shown with an earlier example. However, in certain situations a verbatim psychotherapy report may have certain advantages and it is for this reason that it is reported here.

Theragnostic Report

Case No. 15   Date_______________

Client: (Name)   Age: 19

WAIS Full Scale IQ 130

Protocol (Interview No. 2, in progress)
    Client: . . . she kinda messed up.
    Therapist: In what way?
    Cl. Oh—she—just—messed up.
    Th. Uh, your mother, or—
    Cl. What do you mean about my mother?

Th. You said that *she*—

Cl. Well, she's *too* interested.

Th. You think, that she's overly interested in your tests or what you're doing.

Cl. Everything, you name it.

Th. You think that this is bad.

Cl. Some things.

Th. For example.

Cl. She could stay out of my way a lot (laughed).

Th. So that maybe she's prying too much.

Cl. A little bit.

Th. Do you have any comments about the tests as a whole, that you have taken?

Cl. I thought that the second battery of tests was a lot more to the point—really asked a lot better questions than parts of the first.

Th. What about the test you took last Saturday, with the blocks and all?

Cl. You mean the Wechsler? Well, it was interesting to take and I thought it covered a lot of material in the short time it took, and I don't know what it measures, but—pretty fascinating test!

Th. (*Interprets the test battery to the client and then sums up by saying the following*) . . . the main point here, personality-wise, is that you *really* don't quite seem to care for people as much as you would like for them to believe. And, you may use a pleasing personality in order to manipulate people to get what you want (client laughs) out of—

Cl. Yeah! (laughingly) No way.

Th. —life with more concern for you than for "Joe." See what I mean?

Cl. Yeah.

Th. Uh—

Cl. My parents, that's the way I am with my parents—I can see that.

Th. Have you given much concern to this? Seem to worry you or bother you, or—

Cl. Not really (in amused tone). I never think about it—I just want to get away from my parents—I'm tired of them—I mean— they're alright and everything.

Th. They don't seem to understand your reasonings or motives, or—

Cl. Well, I—you can pick it out pretty well.

Th. You mean me?

Cl. You pick it out—I act pretty well, but I'm doing it just because I have to.

Th. Have you ever had the feeling that the world was run by a type of "jungle philosophy" or the "survival of the fittest"?

Cl. In a way. I think that I'm kinda—my parents, my dad for instance, he doesn't do a lot more than he has to.

Th. You feel this may have influenced your attitudes?

Cl. Might have—uh, he doesn't step on anybody; in fact, he might get stepped on—nobody is going to step on *me*—I feel they *will*, but—

Th. Not if you can prevent it.

Cl. If I can prevent it, I'd be willing to—there's *no way!*

Th. So then, perhaps the means justifies the end?

Cl. Maybe. My dad's a pretty good guy, but he just hadn't—to get anything you have to get, take—really—nothing is given to you.

Th. Should everybody have a chance to have an education; that is, should only the best people be educated?

Cl. We were talking that point in Botany class, I mean in Zoo— the best should be sterilized, I mean *shouldn't* be. The worst should be. I think that everybody should be educated—if you get through the first few grades—if you cut it, you cut it, if you don't, give the tests and say that you take the top seventy per cent and try to work with them; the bottom are pretty out of it, and then as you progress, just the ones that above should just keep getting cut off until you've got a—I mean, uh, that's how they do it in F＿＿＿＿＿. When you're, you take a test and you don't cut it, well they ask you to leave the University or the College—you have to take one every year—and, if you don't cut it you don't cut it.

Th. Getting back to your father, you don't quite look upon your father as being an authoritative figure or anything like that.

Cl. Except at home he is, or work—he's a foreman. He can *express* at work, at home he hadn't acted or said anything about how anything's been carried out, or anything. He feels the more belligerent in his tactics.

Th. Hmmmm.

Cl. Cause *look!* Look at people that are successful! You don't see *them* pushed around too often.

Th. Then do you seem to respect a person in authority for what they can do, or for what they can accomplish through this authority?

Cl. I don't see people get authority, just "pure dee" step on people, I mean, if you get it and they deserve it, well, if they get it and then use it right, well, I look up to them.

Th. Have you ever had the opportunity to do somebody dirty or step on them?

Cl. Yep! I've *done* it too!

Th. In what respect?

Cl. Well, there was this kid who was going to beat me up at the football field, he said, mouthed off a lot. He was in the hospital for about two weeks.

Th. Hmmmm. You kind of lit into him then.

Cl. Yeah.

Th. What do you feel is the reason for certain types of delinquency, say either in actually afflicting physical harm on your rival gang, or innocent bystanders, or vandalism or something along this line?

Cl. Well uh—I wonder what causes a person to want to steal—I know I've wanted to a lot. I mean, it's not, it's not greed, mostly or, trying to get by to pull something on somebody, but I've had my share of mild little things like that. I don't know why I did it —I wanted something.

Th. You feel probably they could do without it.

Cl. Yeah. I could have done without a lot of things; hundreds of little things. The big things—(laughed).

Th. You don't feel it would be too bad, the big things.

Cl. No. (laughed)

Th. What do you consider the big things?

Cl. The bank (laughed). What do *you* consider the big things? (laughed) The store, anything seems to be pretty big—anything over fifty dollars is pretty big—over ten is pretty big in my book. I don't think it would be hard—people are stupid. I mean, as a whole.

Evaluation

This nineteen-year-old college student quite obviously gives an impression of being one who is more concerned for his own existence than for the well being and inherent rights of others. He is quite intelligent and seems to have the ability to self-actualize himself in several appropriate ways. He seems to have a "survival of the fittest" philosophy in a very literal sense which indicates that he would use little restraint in achieving his own ends, whether or not they be socially acceptable or unacceptable.

Diagnosis

Social maladjustment with antisocial features.

Prognosis

Fair.

Recommendations

Since this patient has a strong tendency toward sociopathy he may show a certain resistance to effective psychotherapy. However, it is felt that he should be placed in either group psychotherapy or that his individual sessions be continued. His behavior should be directed toward socially acceptable activities and he should be given a better opportunity to establish his personal identity in life. His high intellectual capacity should enable him to follow higher educational goals which should provide him with a certain amount of self-realization.

(Signed) John Doe, Ph.D.
Psychologist

Four sample psychotherapy reports have been presented in this chapter. Each was different in format and content. From this, the reader should be able to ascertain the direction that reports of this type can take. For the most part, a therapy report will be no more than several sentences in length—a few paragraphs at the most. If reports are made at frequent intervals, such as after each psychotherapy session, brief reports are not only economical in time but are much more practical for the reader.

Another guideline when thinking about the length of a report of therapeutic progress is the amount of interaction which the client undergoes. With some patients who are very nontalkative only one or two sentences may describe their therapeutic interactions. With patients who are frequently seen in therapy one usually writes a short paragraph on each patient at the close of a given psychotherapy session. And, the longest report is not necessarily the best and the most informative.

In some instances, one can obtain a very good picture of the client through a detailed narration as shown by Case No. 15. The spontaneity of this particular client's answers tells a great deal about his thought processes during the course of the one-hour individual psychotherapy session.

Chapter XII

THE COMPREHENSIVE PSYCHOLOGICAL

SEVERAL TYPES of psychological reports have been discussed thus far. Each was rather specific in scope and content. The psychiatric examination, the intellectual evaluation, the personality evaluation, and the treatment summary each have their places in the patient's medical record folder or case file. Not all will be present as separate reports on each client, but most of the information contained in each should be found among the records of most clients. Many times a more thorough and far-reaching report will be the major contribution on a given client or patient. This report is called the *comprehensive psychological.*

The comprehensive psychological report differs from all others in that it includes a great deal of interview, test, medical, and observed behavior data on one's client. Unlike the psychiatric examination which usually takes less than an hour to complete, the comprehensive psychological may take a half day or perhaps a day in order to complete. This is especially true if a large battery of tests are administered. Also, the person preparing the comprehensive report may review the patient's medical record, talk with other psychiatric team members, review therapy notes, and relate other pertinent data within the report.

Any comprehensive psychological evaluation should contain interview data as well as the results of tests of intelligence, organicity, and personality. In some instances tests of interests, aptitudes, or special tests such as sensory measures may be included in the over-all test battery.

During the evaluation process one usually begins with an interview with the patient. Afterwards, the actual testing should begin. A recommended procedure is to administer one each of tests which measure intelligence, organicity, and personality. After having done this, the examiner is in a much better position to decide whether or not additional tests should be administered in order to clarify other data. For example, if the examiner administers a test of organicity and the patient functions in a suspicious manner then the examiner may wish to administer one or more additional tests of organicity in order to better ascertain the nature of the client's functioning. Also, if the examinee is performing inconsistently on a given test, then the examiner may wish to administer another, but similar, test in order to clarify certain areas of performance.

Several types of comprehensive reports will be presented next which indicate different reporting situations and psychologists' approaches. These reports will be divided into two major groups. The first group will concern sample reports that could be used in the school counseling setting; and, the second group will illustrate some clinical reports which might be used in a public or private psychiatric setting. Both groups, however, have certain commonalities of format even though the language and style will tend to vary.

SCHOOL COUNSELING REPORTS

The first counseling report is an abbreviated one which might be adequate in referral situations or where extensive report content is not required for a given case.

Psychological Report

Case No. 16   Date________________

Client: (Name)
Referred by: Miss Jones, Teacher

Tests Administered
Interview
Wechsler Adult Intelligence Scale (WAIS)
Gorham *Proverbs Test*
Guilford-Zimmerman Temperament Survey (GZTS)
School and College Ability Tests (SCAT)
Cooperative English Tests (CET)
Differential Aptitude Tests: VR, SR, MR (DAT)
Watson-Glaser Critical Thinking Appraisal (WGCTA)
Kuder Preference Record, Vocational

Purpose of Evaluation
This twenty-two-year-old single, white male was referred by Miss Jones for a psychological evaluation. He is a junior in college and is having difficulty with his courses; and, he has not selected a major field as yet.

Results of Evaluation
This student possesses an above average intellectual ability with a Full Scale *WAIS* IQ of 117. He evidenced some impaired ability to concentrate on the test, however, especially in subtests requiring calculation skills. On both the *WAIS* and the *Proverbs Test* he displayed an above average ability to deal in abstract concepts. Deductive and interpretative reasoning skills were at the 88th percentile on the *WGCTA*. Mechanical Reasoning was at the 45th; Verbal Reasoning was at the 10th; and Spatial Relations ability was at the 65th percentile on the *DAT*.

His scores on the *CET* were low, with his Total English factor being in the 6-18th percentile range. On the *SCAT*, his Verbal score was low, being in the 25-47th percentile band. Quantitatively, he scored in the 25-45th percentile band, while his total aptitude score on the *SCAT* was in the 28-40 percentile range.

On the *GZTS* he displayed a picture of low motivation, borderline social interaction skills, and conflicts between his personal and other relations.

The *Kuder* indicated high scientific and literary interests. His mechanical, persuasive, and artistic interests were within average limits.

Interpretatively, the client's achievement does not seem to be compatible with his ability level. Namely, he is an underachiever. His learning patterns may be affected by his poor verbal skills such as poor reading speed and level of comprehension. His literary interests which are high do not seem to be realistic, in terms of his verbal scores. However, his high scientific interests seem to be within his ability level providing he can become sufficiently motivated to undertake these endeavors.

Recommendations
Short-term vocational and person counseling is indicated. The client should be seen twice a week, with an emphasis in therapy being placed upon decision-making and problem-solving skills. This approach should better equip this borderline neurotic student to cope with his academic, social, personal, and intellectual assets and liabilities.

(Signed) John Doe, M.Ed.
Counselor

In the report on Case No. 16, neither social nor historical information was discussed. Also, a clinical diagnosis was not given. The next report contains more descriptive "clinical" information. In Case No. 17 the counselor directed his report toward diagnosis of the student's problem and gave suggestions for follow-up.

Psychological Report

Case No. 17   Date________________

Client: (Name)   Age: 15-10

Referred by: Mr. Jones, Teacher, 8th grade.

Reason for Referral

A diagnostic and placement evaluation of this eighth grade student was requested by his teacher. He was seen on ________________, 19_____.

Tests Administered
   Interview
   Wechsler Intelligence Scale for Children (WISC).
   Ammons *Full Range Picture Vocabulary Test* (FRPV).

Behavioral Observations

This student was very cooperative in the testing session but seemed to have below average enthusiasm for the actual testing. The client has a pronounced foreign accent; however, no serious communication problems were experienced. He appeared as a shy boy and volunteered neither information nor informal conversation unless spoken to by the examiner. During the testing activities, he had a pronounced nasal drip which seemed to be due to hay fever; he "sniffed" frequently and did not use a handkerchief.

Social History

He reported that both of his parents are living and that his father is employed as a migratory laborer. He has four brothers, aged 8, 17, 19, and 21. Neither parent graduated from high school. He said that his best subject in school was arithmetic and that he enjoyed playing football.

Intellectual Findings

This student obtained a Verbal IQ of 55, a Performance IQ of 92, and a Full Scale IQ of 70 on the *WISC*. On the *FRPV* test, he obtained a mental age of 8.2 years with a Verbal IQ of 52. Overall, there was a marked impairment in his verbal skills in contrast to his performance skills. He seemed to be functioning at about the third or fourth grade level overall, despite his performance ability being within average limits. His verbal responses showed considerable poverty of content and were much more concrete than abstract. Problem solving ability and deductive reasoning skills were similarly poor. His knowledge and understanding of his environment was poor. Arithmetic was his strongest skill tested; but, it too was below average.

His ability to synthesize parts into meaningful wholes was within low-average limits as was his ability to perform manipulative tasks. When asked to read a passage from a subtest of the *WISC*, he did so in a word-by-word manner which indicated a severe impairment in reading ability.

Personality Indications

This student displayed above average shyness; however, he did not appear to be severely withdrawn. He did seem to lack motivation in the academic areas and tended to feel that others were passing him by. He remarked that at times he felt rejected by the other students. Also, a lack of self-confidence and impaired social skills seem to be prevalent.

Diagnostic Summary

Dull-normal performance intelligence with verbal intelligence being at the moderate mentally retarded level. His maximum intellectual potential seems to be at the low-average area. Pronounced shyness and lack of self-confidence are present. Cultural and educational deprivation seem to be present. No indications of any serious personality malfunction are present.

Recommendations
1. Remedial reading work.
2. Placement in a vocational curriculum.
3. Consider placement in a high school special education unit.
4. Vocational counseling to prepare him for a work role after school.
5. Apprenticeship training.

(Signed) Mary Doe, Ed.D.
Counselor

The report on Case No. 17 was obviously more comprehensive than was the abbreviated report presented on Case No. 16. Where the shorter report was divided into only three sections, the latter contained eight major sections. It goes without saying that the longer report was more meaningful and contained additional information which could better assist the student's teacher in developing an individualized program of study for him. The use of the identifying "headings" in these two reports is optional and tends to make the report content somewhat more easily read.

The next report is more clinically oriented than the other two were. Yet, it is still suited for the school counseling situation (especially at the college level). Again, one must consider the academic orientation of the potential readers of the reports; and, this should be more of a guideline than attempting to specifically designate a form for high school, college, or mental hospital reports per se.

Psychological Report

Case No. 18   Date________________

Client: (Name)

Referred by: Self

This white, single male, aged twenty-three came to see the university counselor on ________________, 19____. He complained that he was having some difficulty with his studies and in his relations with others, especially girls. He was seen today for an interview and psychological testing.

Tests Administered
Interview.
Wechsler Adult Intelligence Scale (WAIS).
Gorham *Proverbs Test.*
School and College Ability Tests (SCAT).
Cooperative English Tests (CET).
Minnesota Multiphasic Personality Inventory (MMPI).
Guilford-Zimmerman Temperament Survey (GZTS).

Medical History
The client stated that he has experienced the usual childhood diseases. At age twenty-one he was informed that he had diabetes mellitus. At the onset of this condition he said he was taking 8 Units of insulin daily and at the present time he is taking 40 Units daily. He presently gives complaints of gastric upsets, anxiety, and fatigue.

Social History
When the client was about four or five years old his mother left his father. He also said that his parents were divorced when he was about twelve or thirteen years old; he subsequently lived with relatives until he entered college. The client emphasized that his rela-

tionship with his mother was much better than with his father. It was also mentioned that his mother and father were "very neurotic" and that his mother had attempted suicide on at least one occasion. He said the family moved around a lot before his parents were divorced and that he never really knew a place he could call home.

During his childhood and school years, he described his social relations as being very unsatisfactory. He said he felt like the "underdog" and that more than once his teachers would punish him for things which he felt were unjust. Around his entrance into the third grade he mentioned that he began "acting up" in class, and would get very upset over trivial happenings. He said that he was considered to be a "sissy" by his male peers up until about age seventeen. At that time he related that he "discarded everything unmasculine and decided to grow up and be a man and destroy all memories of the past." At the same time he remarked that he began to develop a hatred for his father and an indifference toward his mother, despite the fact that the family had been separated for several years due to the divorce.

General Behavioral Observations

This client displays a sad, lonely, and dejected facial expression. He stoops as he walks as if he were trying to "pull himself away" from his environment. He speaks in a low monotone and little spontaneity in his conversation is elicited. The client smoked during the interview and subsequent testing.

Psychometric Evaluation

On the *WAIS* he obtained a Verbal IQ of 124, a Performance IQ of 116, and a Full Scale IQ of 112. A high level of conceptual organization ability and whole-part synthesis was shown. Intratest and intertest variability was minimal but nevertheless present. His power of concentration was below average as was his ability to perform mental calculations on command. On both the *WAIS* and the *Proverbs Test* he displayed a high level of ability to reason abstractly. On the *SCAT* he displayed superior verbal reasoning ability (82-93 percentile band) with a very low ability in quantitative areas (0-4 percentile band). On the *CET* his Total English score was within the 57-81 percentile band which was compatible with his verbal score on the *SCAT*.

Personality indications on the *GZTS* show a person who is introverted, depressed, more given to thought than action, and one who has a low drive level. On the *MMPI* he presents himself as a person with an over-concern with bodily functions, and an immature approach to adult problem-solving. Strong feelings of depression, manifested in pessimism, feelings of uselessness, a tendency to worry, and dejection in general are shown. He seems to be a person who has difficulty in profiting effectively from experience—he mentioned that he has had considerable difficulty in his relationships with employers. Additionally, he seems to have an above average amount of suspiciousness as well as a tendency toward feelings of persecution. This student also seems to have a high degree of unexpressed hostility toward himself and others. In the social realm, he appears to have a great amount of difficulty in interpersonal relations and tends to withdraw from others.

Diagnosis
Neurotic Depressive Reaction.

Prognosis
Good for present episode; uncertain for future episodes.

Recommendations
Intensive individual psychotherapy; daily one-half hour sessions are recommended. Physical examination and possible use of anti-depressant drugs concurrent with psychotherapy. Therapy sessions should be directed toward tasks of problem-solving, and ways of establishing more meaningful social relations. Educational and vocational counseling would be helpful. Even though this client seems to be currently more psychoneurotic than psychotic, it is felt that he has a strong disposition toward a more severe and psychotic personality. Therefore, intensive crisis oriented psychotherapy as well as preventive psychotherapy should be incorporated into any therapy sessions.

(Signed) John Doe, Ph.D.
Counseling Psychologist

Case No. 18 was written up with more of a "clinical" view than were the other counseling cases. This case report was functionally divided into seven sections, the last one including the Diagnosis, Prognosis, and Recommendations. The material for this report was condensed from some ten pages of interview transcript as well as several pages of test data. To include all of this detailed information in a psychological report would have made for an excessively long report. This has been demonstrated with Cases 10 and 15. If extensive, detailed information must be included in the report (including the actual test answer sheets), then it should be filed as a supplement in the medical record or case folder.

The psychological report should similarly not be used to dupli-
cate the client's entire record in one comprehensive report as one
could easily write one or two pages on the results of each test
that was administered as well as several pages describing the
therapist-client interactions during a given psychotherapy interview session. In fact, the competent psychological examiner
could have probably arrived at the diagnosis of "Neurotic
Depressive Reaction" in Case No. 18 from the interview data
alone, or from a single psychometric profile such as the *MMPI*.
Frankly, the statement, "this client displays a sad, lonely, and
dejected facial expression," would tend to support a diagnosis of
depression.

The reader should remember that no single case presented in
this book will include all of the possible points of information
previously outlined. All cases illustrated here, as well as in actual
practice, will be different; and, certain points are emphasized
and used in some reports and not in others. The nature of the
actual case will determine the information to be included in any
given psychological report.

CLINICAL REPORTS

The difference between the school counseling report and the
clinical report is mainly in the language and the reading audience.
Also, different types of recommendations for treatment may be
indicated in each type of report. With the counseling report,
teachers, principals, other counselors, and similar individuals will
usually be the primary readers. Clinical reports will usually be
read by physicians, clinical psychologists, nurses, psychiatric
rehabilitation workers, and others who have access to the client's
medical record folder in a psychiatric facility.

There is a general tendency to avoid the use of clinical, diagnostic labels (such as "schizophrenic, manic-depressive," and the
like) in the school counseling setting. One reason for this is that
it acts as a precaution against a parent or other lay person reading or hearing of the label and subsequently attaching too much
significance to its obscure meaning. Clinical and counseling professionals alike are aware of the problems in diagnosing and the
actual or implied meaning of diagnoses. Therefore, in the ele-

mentary and secondary school settings in particular, the use of traditional clinical diagnostic labels should be avoided. However, traditional diagnoses are more common in the college or university and out-patient or in-patient mental health facilities.

Essentially, all psychological reports should convey the same information about the client irrespective of the professional climate. Facts are facts and subjective opinions are subjective. This is to say that the client's test responses, interview disclosures, and similar information should be reported in any report. Inversely, the information will be written up in different language styles and levels of professional jargon for different major reading audiences. If it is necessary to prepare a psychological report for two vastly different audiences, such as for a parent and for another psychologist, then the writer should write *two* reports. The report for the parent (or spouse) should be written in common sense, everyday language terms; the one for the other psychologist (or similar professional) should be written in more detailed, clinical language. However, one should not construe this to mean that one should have free license to write in total psychological jargon—this is taboo!

Case No. 19 will illustrate two types of reports, each on the same person. The first report is written to the referring physician; the second to the client's wife. Both communicate essentially the same thing. One could send the "wife's report" to the physician; however, he might feel insulted. On the other hand, a report such as the one to the physician *should never* be sent to the wife (or parent, or other lay person).

Psychological Report

Case No. 19   Date________________

Client: (Name)

Referred by: Dr. Smith

This thirty-five-year-old white, married male was referred to the Midtown Psychological Clinic for an intellectual and personality evaluation by his personal physician, Dr. Smith. The client was seen on ________________, 19____, for this evaluation.

The client appeared as a well-mannered, well-groomed man who appeared his stated age. He was very cooperative with the examiner. During the interview and subsequent testing activities he displayed few overt emotions and spoke in an unspontaneous monotone.

The following medical and social history was revealed by the client. He comes from a family of seven; he has four brothers. Both parents are living at the present time. The usual childhood diseases as well as lobar pneumonia were experienced. When the client was about twelve years old he was run over by a playmate's wagon and subsequently fell on his head; medical treatment was necessary. However, he denied any recollection of high fever, blackout spells, dizziness, or unexplained nausea and vomiting resulting from this injury. He stated that he drinks socially but no alcoholic addiction was admitted.

His relations with others were reported to be satisfactory and that he did not have much difficulty in getting along with people. In school he said that he made average grades but had some trouble with written reports, algebra, and geometry. He did mention, however, that he had some difficulty while serving in the Army; a medical discharge ensued.

The client married when he was seventeen years old. He has two children and one on the way. Going further, he mentioned that he has been having some problems with his wife; and, he feels that he "married her out of sympathy." When queried about this, he said that she was "not well." He changed the subject and said that "one time I went to a bar with another guy, instead of reporting to work, and when I returned home my wife was just coming in from somewhere . . . wife plays around on me." He then said that an argument ensued and that he and his wife slapped each other once; then he remarked, "but—I don't like fighting." As a child, "kids used to try to fight me, or get somebody else in a fight." Changing the subject again, he said, "one time I attempted suicide, but I wouldn't try it again, unless I try to kill myself by smoking—maybe subconsciously I want to kill myself, but not consciously. I've had an unhappy childhood; it's been worse since I got married. My wife's been sick . . . my father encouraged us kids to fight; when I got my arm broke, I was scared of what my father was going to do. He got mad . . . my father used to call me '________________,' and I never did like that, or even the name, '________________.'"

He was asked if he had ever heard, seen, or felt any unusual sensations. His reply was that "I started going to the ________________ church after I got married and 'was saved' but I didn't feel any different." Going further, he stated that "when I had the nervous breakdown [he was admitted to a general hospital where he received electroshock treatments] I went for treatment and felt 'saved' after that." When asked, "What were your thoughts about the time you had the nervous breakdown?," he replied, "Well, I usually sleep mornings—when I got up in time to have enough time in the mornings and when I got to work they were taking up a collection for someone in the office—I put one dollar in the collection—my mind was racing a mile a minute and my hands began to shake a lot when I thought about going home to see this man. I went home."

When asked about his wife, the client said, "my wife feels tired a lot, mild case of epilepsy, feels tired, and had four C-sections in childbirth. I feel tired a lot—get about seven hours sleep a night. Have trouble getting to sleep. Get depressed over bills, and whether or not I am going to Heaven or not, and past nervous breakdown."

Psychometric Results

On the *Wechsler Adult Intelligence Scale* (WAIS), he received a Verbal IQ of 114, a Performance IQ of 101, and a Full Scale IQ of 109. His highest scaled scores were 14 and 15 on the *Information* and *Vocabulary* subtests, respectively, which indicated an intellectual potential in the above average area. His Verbal IQ was 13 points higher than his Performance IQ thereby indicating either a) a schizophrenic process, b) a high level or anxiety and depression, or c) borderline organicity. Organicity was ruled out due to his average scores in the performance areas. A low score on the *Graham-Kendall Memory for Designs* test tended to support the absence of any intracranial pathology.

Inter-test variability on the *WAIS* was pronounced with scaled scores ranging from 7 to 15. Similarly, some intra-test variability was shown, especially on the *Similarities* subtest. These variabilities indicate a schizophrenic process in operation. On the whole, his *WAIS* profile evidenced a lowered ability to function in areas requiring immediate psychomotor effort, suggestive of a) depression, and b) lowered motivation.

The quality of the client's answers to the six verbal subtests reflected a person who has read a great deal and who seems to have a good command of the English language despite his tenth grade formal education. For the most part, this man is a person who tends to overelaborate his answers—he gives multiple explanations and definitions to words and questions. Also, bizarre answers were given on several test items. Hostility was likewise implied in his definition of the word "impale" where he said, "pin to, thrust a sword into someone, impaled on a spear." Several rejections of items were noted, indicating a certain degree of negativism, hostility, or lowered motivation.

On the *Minnesota Multiphasic Personality Inventory* (MMPI) the client obtained a profile code of 8426731 ' 9 (73) 6:15:13 where his two high points, *84*, strongly suggest the presence of a schizophrenic process in operation. His score on the *Depression* subscale is also high which is suggestive of a continuance of his self-devaluing feelings from before. There is also evidenced a high level of feelings of suspiciousness, and ideas of grandeur and persecution. The *MMPI* profile further indicates a man who has trouble in decision-making. His depressed psychomotor functioning was brought out in his taking five hours to complete the test which is about three hours above average.

Diagnosis
Schizophrenic reaction, paranoid type, with reactive depression.

Prognosis
Guarded.

Recommendations
This man should undergo extensive group and individual psychotherapy accompanied by chemotherapy. He should be referred to a vocational rehabilitation counselor for employment planning. It is also recommended that this man be admitted to a private or public psychiatric facility for a period of at least ninety days, since his condition is one warranting immediate action. Out-patient treatment does not seem to be adequate at this time.

(Signed) Mary Jones, Ph.D.
Consulting Psychologist

The reader will undoubtedly note that in the clinical report on Case No. 19 that the body of the report consisted of two major sections, *viz.* the interview and the psychometric evaluation. This was an arbitrary division for a functional reason—the over-all evaluation served as a) a mental status psychiatric examination, and b) a psychometric evaluation. Both were incorporated into a single, comprehensive psychological report. In the interview section there are several places where dialogue is represented. This inclusion of dialogue was done so that a reader could get a better idea of the thought processes which this client was experiencing. The use of dialogue tends to illustrate the fragmented and bizarre thinking of this man much better than the psychologist's comments alone could have done.

A report of this man's status was also requested by his *wife*. This is not a routine situation. Nevertheless, the psychologist accommodated her and presented a report as follows in *lay terms* and much abbreviated.

Psychological Report

Case No. 19   Date_______________

Client: (Name)

To: Mrs._________________   Relationship: Wife

Your husband, Mr._______________, was seen on _______________, 19_____, for a psychological evaluation at the request of your family physician, Dr. Smith.

Your husband was very cooperative and displayed a pleasing manner during the evaluation. He related to the examiner his medical and childhood history and his present family situation. He seems to feel that he is having difficulty in communicating his status as a husband and as a father to his wife and children. Additionally, he seems to feel some conflict over his religious beliefs and whether or not he is satisfied over his salvation. He also tends to have worries over his previous hospitalization at _______________ Hospital and wonders whether or not others may look down upon him for having been there. He is also quite worried over his job situation and becomes distressed when the monthly bills began to accumulate.

Intellectually, he is of average to above average intelligence which indicates that he has the ability to finish his high school education and, if he desires, to attend a college or university. His worries tend to impair his ability to think and to perform intellectual tasks. He has a good command of the English language which would indicate that he could function adequately in an academic situation. Your husband is having a great deal of difficulty in coping with his frustrations and anxieties and more times than not feels quite inadequate over any failures he may experience. These problems seem to greatly impair his ability to make decisions as well as his relations with his family and associates.

Recommendations

Mr._______________ is definitely in need of short-term psychiatric care in a private or public psychiatric facility for at least thirty to ninety days. It is felt that out-patient visits to a clinic would not be comprehensive and intensive enough at this time to provide him with the immediate care which he needs. There is every reason to believe that he will be able to return to his family and friends, greatly improved, if he accepts treatment and adheres to the intensive therapeutic regime. I would additionally recommend that both you and your husband participate in a series of weekly marriage counseling sessions (during his hospitalization and perhaps after) in order that each of you may achieve a better understanding of one another's feelings, needs, and goals in life.

(Signed) Mary Jones, Ph.D.
Consulting Psychologist

Each report on Case No. 19 said approximately the same thing. The first was of a clinical nature and the second was a lay report to the client's wife. The second report had several significant points. First, it was written in common sense or layman's language with a strict avoidance of any clinical terms or diagnoses. Secondly, there was an avoidance of test scores and IQ results since these are types of diagnostic labels in themselves. Thirdly, there was an emphasis upon the client's *assets*, while at the same time, not minimizing his liabilities. Fourthly, it was stressed that even though this man was not "stark-raving mad," he did need immediate treatment and that it should be short-term institutionalization, not out-patient care. And, fifthly, there was a recommendation that both the client *and* his wife come in for marital counseling since it was felt that his spouse could a) achieve a better understanding of her husband's problems, and b) be more qualified to act as an agent of prevention.

The use of a layman's report need not be limited to the clinical setting. At times one may be requested by an interested parent of an elementary, secondary, or college level student. If possible, a layman's report should be discouraged—the parent or spouse should be seen in person and the case discussed with them. But, if a report must be sent, it should be written in lay terms and without clinical technicalities and psychological jargon. In any event, unless the client is a child, the clinician should obtain a release of confidential information form from the client before a report such as this is sent.

The next clinical report, Case No. 20, was made on a client who had been referred for evaluation due to suspected brain damage. Brain damage was suspected by the client's physician (in addition to a behavioral problem) and the psychological examination was requested prior to the running of an electroencephalogram (brain wave test). The reason for this examination was two-fold. First, the client lived a long distance from the nearest facility possessing an electroencephalograph; and, second, since psychological tests could indicate personality as well as gross organic problems (for diagnostic support in this case), the psychological evaluation was chosen by the physician as an initial step in this case.

Psychological Report

Case No. 20   Date________________

Client: (Name)

Referred by: Dr. Jones

Reason for referral: Suspected behavioral problems secondary to brain damage.

This twenty-one-year-old white, single male was referred by Dr. Jones to the State Psychiatric Clinic for a psychological examination. The client was seen on ________________, 19____.

A pretesting interview revealed a well-groomed, well-mannered young man in seemingly good physical condition. His speech was somewhat slurred and hard to understand. Mental status examination revealed a man who has a fairly good memory for recent and past events. He denies any history of physical trauma, or of alcoholic or drug addiction. He is oriented as to time, place, and person. Above average overt anxiety in the form of trembling hands, perspiration on his forehead, and a look of fear upon his face was present at the time of the interview. His emotional tone was bland and flat and little spontaneity was shown. He stated that he had experienced the usual childhood diseases. Suicidal or homicidal fantasies were generally denied by the client, even though he did say that he would at times become very despondent when things did not go his way.

When asked about his past employment, peer relations, and family interactions, he said, "My old man (his step-father) said I wasn't trustful." In terms of employment, he had been unable to hold a job for any length of time; and, most of his work experience had been at odd jobs. He had been dishonorably discharged from the military for reasons he would not disclose to the examiner. Going further he related that his grades in school had been poor (D's and F's) and that he quit school as a sophomore. The client began talking about his nerves and said, "while at work I got awful nervous . . .

just don't like to work . . . was going with this girl at home, then got into service . . . while in the service got awful lonesome." Then he commented that, ". . . stomach feels like all in tension—tied in a knot . . . sometimes I get dizzy when I bend down and raise up fast."

On the intellectual examination, a Verbal IQ of 80 on the Ammons *Quick Test* was obtained. However, a Verbal IQ of 88, a Performance IQ of 81, and a Full Scale IQ of 84 on the *Wechsler Adult Intelligence Scale* (WAIS) was obtained. On the *WAIS* there was considerable inter-test variability with scaled scores ranging from 4 to 11. Similarly, there was a large amount of intra-test variability. These fluctuations indicated a) an absence of idiopathic mental deficiency, since he obtained four average scores; and b) an indication of schizophrenic patterning. Furthermore, several easy items were missed as well as erratic performance on the more difficult items. His verbal responses were very concrete, rambling, negativistic, and at times bizarre. He gave up easily and had to be encouraged to continue on several occasions. More than once he gave "opposites" (a schizophrenic tendency) to some items on two of the subtests of the *WAIS*. Average ability was shown in his ability to do mental calculations, concentrate on effort, learn new tasks and to distinguish between essential and nonessential details. He performed at the dull-normal level in terms of general environmental information, comprehension of social phenomena, and the execution of psychomotor tasks. His ability to deal with abstract concepts, and to size up social situations was at the mild mentally deficient level; while his vocabulary usage and performance on part-whole synthesis tasks were at the moderately retarded level. Of special interest was an intellectual deterioration quotient of 50 per cent.

Organically, the client showed some deviant signs on the *WAIS*, in terms of psychomotor performance. On the *Bender Visual-Motor Gestalt Test* his reproductions were well preserved and proportioned; however, he rotated design A by 180 degrees. Some lack of effort and perseverance were shown in his drawings. All designs were correctly oriented (except A) and no classic signs of organicity were elicited, other than this one rotation. Since some cases of organicity can have good, specialized test performance in some areas and not in others, the possibility of intracranial pathology is not entirely ruled out with this client.

Comment

This client has inconsistent symptomology and test performance at the very least. On the other hand, he performed somewhat consistently in the low-normal to borderline retarded intellectual level. From one standpoint, he displays several signs of intracranial pathology while from another, he does not. On interview, personality indications are that of an anxious, and somewhat confused man; however, test findings indicate verbal responses which are characteristically of a schizophrenic nature. There is also a speech disturbance which may be secondary to an emotional problem; the possibility of a tumor in Broca's region should not be overlooked. Since this client has no history of psychiatric treatment and since he is in fairly good contact with reality, a psychotic disorder seems less of a reality than a pre-psychotic manifestation.

Diagnosis

Personality disorder, schizoid type, with anxiety reaction. Rule out brain syndrome.

Prognosis

Guarded.

Recommendations

This man should definitely have an electroencephalogram made. There are indications that there is a presence of a degenerative type of intracranial pathology. Additionally, the use of psychotrophic drugs should be considered for control of his manifest anxiety. Extensive individual or group psychotherapy is recommended. This man should be administered the electroencephalogram at the earliest possible date, with psychotherapy immediately following. After participating in therapy for ninety days he should be reevaluated.

> (Signed) Mary Jones, Ph.D.
> Consulting Psychologist

In Case No. 20 no major report headings were used except "Comment, diagnosis, prognosis, and recommendations." Again, this is a variation to use in report writing. Also, the reports on Cases 19 and 20 did not use a listing of "Tests Administered" at the beginning of the reports. This arrangement is at the discretion of the clinician. A new section, *Comment*, was used on the last report. This entry may be used for any number of situations such as a summary, conclusion, addendum, or in the instance of Case No. 20, a rationale for a diagnosis. The Comment section could also be used as a place to justify a multiple diagnosis, since one would not ordinarily use more than one diagnostic statement without a sufficient reason.

The reader will further note that in the clinical reports on Cases 19 and 20, interpretative statements were given following certain test findings. A writing technique such as this is often used to further clarify certain findings in interview and test data.

The comprehensive psychological examination is usually considered to be one where both interview and psychometric data are incorporated into the report. Also, case history or medical report data may be included. Unless several types of source information are included in this report form, one can hardly consider it to be of a "comprehensive" nature. Conversely, a skilled clinician can perhaps obtain a vast amount of information from a client on an interview alone; and, in some cases it may be more thorough than through the administration of a number of tests. But, most of us do not possess perfection in interviewing. For the purposes of definition, comprehensiveness is intended here to denote the conducting of an interview, the referring to the client's past record (if there is one), and the administration and analysis of several types of psychological tests for inclusion in the written report.

Chapter XIII

COMPUTER APPLICATIONS IN PSYCHOLOGICAL REPORTING

HISTORY OF THE COMPUTER

For a number of years the need for the construction of an automated calculating device was prevalent. The so-called "modern" calculators were being developed in the 17th century; however, little progress was made until the 19th century. In the 1830's Charles Babbage made the first attempt to build a *computer* which he called an "analytic engine" for use in the tabulation of statistical data (Pia, 1964). This clumsy machine was a failure as far as computers go; however, his *computing principle* has been retained in more recent technological endeavors. In 1888 an alphanumeric coding system and a tabulating machine for use with punched card systems was developed by Herman Hollerith; and, the code came to be known as the *Hollerith Code*. Hollerith was able to implement his system for the 1890 United States Census data; furthermore, his coding system is being used extensively in data processing applications today.

The Burroughs Corporation marketed the first mechanical calculating machine in 1885; yet, this machine was not a "computer" by modern definition. The first truly modern automatic (not to be confused with total automation as no computer is able to operate *en toto* without human intervention) computer was built at Harvard University for the United States Navy in 1944. *Magnetic relays* were used in this device to perform computerized calculations. Later, in World War II, the first *vacuum tube* computer was developed by the Univac Corporation at the University of Pennsylvania (Honeywell, 1964).

There are essentially two basic types of computers that have been developed. The first, an *analog* system which answers questions of "how much?"; and, the *digital* computer which answers questions of "how many?" The analog type performs calculations in terms of physical analogies such as similarly achieved with the slide rule, speedometer, or hourglass. The digital types uses a numerical code system in its data representation and performs mathematical analyses on these numerically represented data. Adding machines, the abacus, punched-card accounting machines, and most computers are digital in principle and operation (Honeywell, 1964).

Three "generations" of computers have been developed since the onset of World War II. The *first* generation series operated on the basis of the previously mentioned vacuum tube component, similar to those used in radios and televisions. These vacuum tube computers were both physically cumbersome and slow (the earlier magnetic relay computers were even slower) by our modern computing standards. The *second* generation of computers used *solid state* components (transistors and other microcircuitry) and were significantly improved over their first generation predecessors. In recent years a *third* generation series has been developed and is an even greater refinement of the second generation technology—some fifty thousand microtransistors can be placed into a common sewing thimble. This latter series is able to read, compute, store, and print data at extremely rapid speeds; thus, calculation times are thought of in terms of millionths of a second intervals.

An elaborate discussion of *how* a computer works internally is entirely out of the scope of this chapter. At the most basic level, a computer "computes" data by use of hundreds of thousands of internal pieces of circuitry, many of which must be assembled under "operating room" cleanliness by using special microscopes to hand-assemble the components. This elaborate system of electronics enables the computer to "read" holes in punched cards or magnetic spots or characters on magnetic tape, special magnetic discs, or optical marks on answer sheets, and other printed forms. Essentially, every single computation or operation within the computer functions in an "all or nothing" fashion. That is, each unit of datum is represented as either a "1-bit" or a "0-bit" state in the electronic circuitry. This is much like the "on" or "off" position or state of an electric light switch or bulb. And, this "yes" and "no" condition is the binary numerical system of data representation. Each hole in a punched card or each magnetic spot on a piece of magnetic tape, on an area of magnetic disc or drum is called a *bit*. One or more *bits* are used to represent a given numeral or alphabet character on a small area of a card, disc, tape, or drum as well as within the computer itself.

To project into the future of the computer, one computer manufacturer predicted that the computer of the 21st century would use chemical configurations (special molecular structures) to store in the vicinity of two million bits of alphabetic and numeric data on the surface the size of a dime. Complementary to this futuristic computer (which, incidentally, is in the developmental stage as of the writing of this book) is the use of a low-powered laser beam which would allow the computer to read data into its memory banks at the rate of *100 million bits* of information *per second* (*Data Process Mag*, 1967, p. 10).

Contrary to lay beliefs, the computer *cannot think* on its own. The computer can only do what a human being *instructs* it to do in a step by step fashion through the use of a *program* which is a series of operating instructions. If it is erroneously instructed, then it will perform erroneous calculations and produce inaccurate results. In the profession this is known by a maxim, "GIGO," or "Garbage *In*—Garbage *Out*." Without the assistance from man, the computer is little more than an expensive, *dumb piece of hardware* which does not even have sufficient innate "intelligence" to start and stop itself. However, with instructions from man telling it *when, why, what,* and *how*, the computer can perform mathematical and logical calculations at speeds which will defy the imagination.

COMPUTER APPLICATIONS IN PSYCHOLOGY

Computer systems are rapidly finding extensive applications into psychological evaluation areas. In fact, computerization of psychological data is quite established in the testing and research areas. Without the use of high-speed digital computers, test results gathered from nationwide samples would take months, if not years to analyze manually.

To appreciate the application of a modern computer system,

consider for a moment the length of time it would take ten psychometricians to score, calculate the means, standard deviations, percentiles, and intercorrelations of two groups of fifty thousand tests, each having ten separate subscores. Under *optimal* processing speeds, an optical scanning device (reads special pencil marks on answer or other data sheets) could read the marks made by the examinees on their answer sheets at 1,000 or more sheets per minute. The scoring and other statistical calculations could be performed within a few minutes. Then, the data results (or a listing of each examinee's scores) could be printed onto a continuous form of paper at 1,000 or more lines per minute. The computer's read-calculate-write operations on these 100,000 tests could be achieved in about one and a half to two hours, excluding "turn around time" spent loading test answer sheets into the optical scanner, print-out paper into the printer, and so forth. It could very probably take the ten psychometricians several weeks to perform these operations using conventional, hand calculating methods.

A case in point is where the author was analyzing an experimental test. A computer system was used to calculate frequency distributions, means, standard deviations, the variance, skewness, and kurtosis on several data samples. Additionally, ninety Fisher's *t* tests, fourteen four-way analyses of variance, and one hundred Pearsonian coefficients of correlation were computed. An orthogonal varimax factor analysis was also conducted with the extraction of four principal factor components. These analyses consumed only a very few minutes of actual computer calculation time (less than ten minutes, in fact) with only a few more minutes being needed to print out the fifty-three page statistical report. Anyone who has worked any statistical problems by hand will appreciate this speed in calculation. The new IBM 360 series of computers has even more fantastic calculation times, as well as other types of computers.

Other psychological uses of computers revolve around the maintenance of patient behavioral and medical reports, patient statistics, including treatment methods, admission and discharge data, diagnostic groupings, and socioeconomic and demographic factors. Treatment and program models are similarly being analyzed by computers, with simulation models being undertaken. A simulation model is where the researcher plugs certain data into the computer and then manipulates different variables in a problem-solving strategy. The simulation model approach is also being used in the study of factors in the area of bionuclear medicine.

Some State hospitals and clinics for the mentally ill are currently using sophisticated computer programs to write patient behavioral records, medical reports, psychological reports, and progress notes in narrative style. It should be pointed out, however, that a fairly large and multipurpose computer system is needed to produce *narrative* reports with any degree of success, since an extensive "dictionary" of statements must be stored into the computer's memory in order to facilitate narrative writing procedures.

COMPUTERIZED MENTAL HEALTH PROJECTS

Some of the applications of computerization in mental health areas include the storing of medical record information, scoring and interpretation of psychological tests and rating scales, analysis of psychotherapy processes, and the reporting of nursing observations and ward behaviors among patients. Also, the evaluation of overall mental health programs is being done (Glueck, 1965a).

Several forms of data input are used in these computer systems. *Punched cards* are a common way by which coded data are read into the computers. The cards may be reused for future processing runs, or the data can be read onto magnetic tapes, discs, or drums for longer-term storage. *Optical-scan* sheets are also very useful in reporting behavioral, medical, and psychotherapeutic data. The examinee or rater merely checks the appropriate item or marks special spaces on the answer sheet or data form which corresponds to the desired information to be processed. Then, the optical scanner "reads" these marks and in turn either a) punches cards with the information encoded, or b) relays the data direct to the computer memory by communication lines, or c) records the data on magnetic tapes, discs, or drums.

Another input source is that of *teleprocessing* whereby on-line terminals (input equipment) in remote stations (any physical location in a building) use special typewriters, telephones, and teleprinters to transmit input data to the central computer console via direct lines of communication. Teleprocessing is used, for example, with a typewriter located at a nursing station with an on-line communication cable leading to the hospital's data processing center. Teleprocessing can also be used long distance, between institutions and between even longer range geographical localities as well as among facilities utilizing computer time-sharing services.

Through these input sources just described the reporting of raw data into the computer is achieved very rapidly. In these systems one can also retrieve processed data at any given moment, especially if the computer has *random access storage.* With random access capability in a computer system, one can retrieve specific information within a group of data at any given point in time. That is, random access capability is achieved through the use of disc packs (resembling a stack of hi-fi records) or magnetic drums, where a read-write "head" can quickly go to a given "address" in the storage area thereby "randomly selecting" a given item or group of data. Random access is contrasted with *sequential access* where the latter method is characteristic of magnetic tape storage—one must search through many data (similar to selecting a passage on a common tape recorder) before one arrives at the desired data. Therefore, by using random access methods, all pertinent patient data can be stored and later retrieved quickly for a given patient or group of patients. This method is especially useful where data must be obtained at any given point in time for on-going treatment and evaluation purposes (Glueck, 1965b).

Until the middle of 1962 little progress had been made in the development of computerized systems in the mental hospital setting. In June of 1962, Camarillo (California) State Hospital spurred the movement toward computerization in this innovative area. In 1963, the Institute of Living in Hartford, Connecticut, began work in the clinical evaluation of mental patient data with the *Minnesota Multiphasic Personality Inventory* and the *Minnesota-Hartford Personality Assay,* among other media.

Shortly thereafter Rockland (New York) State Hospital computerized a Mental Status Examination, a Developmental History, and a Psychiatric Questionnaire. Later, Rockland developed a general purpose computer program called SCRIBE (*S*ystematic, *C*omplete, *R*etrievable, *I*nterlingual, *B*rief, *E*xpandable) which was designed to produce narrative reports from any "check list" of input media. Additionally, Tulane University in New Orleans worked on a patient profile retrieval system (Crowley, 1967).

When the Camarillo State Hospital implemented their program they emphasized several evaluation areas. The first area encompassed information about specific patients which was obtained from behavioral rating scales and the like. Second was an application of clinical research data. As a tertiary feature, Camarillo has been evaluating intact subsystems (wards, units, etc.) within the hospital; and, fourth, inter-institutional program evaluations were begun (Graetz, 1966).

The Institute of Living was continuing their computer applications in the meantime. Here, they began to produce better and more sophisticated nursing notes than previously achieved, as well as refining their input methodology. Special checklist forms were used to "chart" patient behavior at the close of each nursing shift. Later, the nurses' observations were sent to the computer center even more frequently, thereby providing for current information retrieval capability at any given time during the day or night. Improved staff observations of patient behavior, reporting procedures, and the standardization of certain reporting terminology were achieved. These accomplishments, in part, led to more feasible and implementable statistical analyses of patient data as well as improved in-service educative models (Rosenberg and Carriker, 1966; Rosenberg, Glueck, and Bennett, 1967). Moreover, the Institute of Living has been able to analyze more efficiently longitudinal patient progress, compare patient progress in terms of individual versus group interactions, compare diagnostic rationale, ascertain "normal" behavioral configurations among hospitalized patients, analyze cyclic behavioral changes, and evaluate the ramifications and effects of patient behavior due to psychotherapy (Rosenberg, Glueck, and Stroebel, 1967).

At the Colorado State Hospital in Pueblo, a "five-year plan" of statewide program evaluation was begun. Community mental health planning was also included in the project. Time studies of staff work loads, analyses of research and training effectiveness, and therapeutic program evaluation were undertaken in this project (Cheney, 1967).

The Reiss-Davis Clinic for Child Guidance in Los Angeles developed the Psychiatric Case History Event System (PsyCHES) which evaluated the totality of the patient's behavioral and medical status. A lexicon was developed to categorize and subsequently code specific *events* so that they could be reported to the computer in machine-readable form. This system was particularly useful where input data were received in heterogeneous ways (Eiduson, Brooks, and Motto, 1966).

The aforementioned on-going projects in the mental health treatment area are only a sample of the more significant projects reported in the literature to date. Any number of special projects are currently underway throughout the United States. Newer programs will most assuredly evolve in time.

It is almost essential for a research and program evaluation model to be philosophically and concretely present in the mental health facility before a component of that model, such as the psychological report, can be computerized. Since computer systems in mental health agencies are relatively new to the mental health care field, one can readily understand why it will be several years before the computerized psychological report will become a routine and commonplace event. Of course, not all hospitals and clinics (especially private practitioners) will have computers and a data processing staff. However, computer service companies can provide these specialized, time-sharing services for a fee. At any rate, there will still be manually written reports, especially in the case of a new patient admission—a report may be needed before a client's record can be set up on the computer.

THE COMPUTERIZED REPORT

Both Rockland State Hospital and the Institute of Living have been making extensive use of the computerized report. In recapitulation, some of these reports include a Mental Status

Examination, a General Purpose Psychiatric Questionnaire, a Developmental History, Nursing Notes, a Comprehensive Patient Observation Report, a Patient Progress Note, a *Minnesota Multiphasic Personality Inventory* printout, and the *Minnesota-Hartford Personality Assay.* Each of these instruments uses a special optical-scan answer sheet which can be directly read by an optical scanning device. Since all of the data items that the examinee or rater marks are done on a special form, the data can be quickly processed by the computer. The information thus read by the computer is subsequently stored in the computer's memory media for later information retrieval. However, one drawback in the use of the optical-scan forms is the problem of extraneous pencil or pen marks being present. To reduce these problems one usually either a) visually scans each sheet for these marks, or b) attempts to instruct persons who fill out the forms to be especially cautious in their use.

The traditional psychological report has been and is one whereby the clinician obtains relevant information on a client from various sources and then writes a narrative report. With a report such as this, the clinician is free to vary the report format, language, and other components at will. Therefore, a very personalized and unique report can be prepared relatively easy on each client. No special forms are necessary—only a pencil and a sheet of scratch paper at the least. With the traditional, manually prepared report the clinician can write a rough draft, revise it, and revise it again as easily as using an eraser or a wastebasket. He can even write the report, type it himself, and have a finished report very quickly without his depending upon anyone else, if necessary. Sound simple? Yes. But, the average clinician will probably spend from one to two hours writing up a comprehensive psychological report with an additional thirty minutes to an hour spent for someone to type it.

This is where the computerized psychological report is useful. A point to keep in mind is that psychologists can conduct both psychotherapy and write reports; however, computers can only write reports—they cannot do conventional psychotherapy as yet. However, Starkweather (1968) reports that experimental work is being done in using computers to conduct simulated psychotherapy interviews. This is meritous; however, whether or not the computer will ultimately replace the traditional psychotherapist is rather questionable at this time. At any rate, assuming that the clinician has access to a computer which has been programmed to write psychological reports, he can, by using a special "answer sheet," mark any combination of several standardized statements on the sheet in a matter of a few minutes. The computer takes over from here by converting these marks to correspond to preprogrammed narrative statements and in turn printing out a narrative report.

Special Reports

The *Mental Status Examination* is a routine multipurpose screening evaluation usually given to each new admission to a psychiatric hospital or clinic. As you probably recall from other chapters, this examination is synonymous with the psychiatric examination. On this examination a large repertoire of data is ultimately collectable on the patient at the time of his evaluation. At this point, the psychiatrist, psychologist, social worker, or other responsible person talks with the patient, observes him, reviews any previous medical history, and then during (or after) the interview makes notes on the patient's mental status. In a computer application, a special form which can be optically-scanned may be used.

Figure 4 illustrates one type of optical scan input form used for a Mental Status Examination. This form lists some major categories of mental status such as demographic data, physical status, emotional thresholds, and areas of social interaction. After the proper spaces on the form have been marked, the optical scanning device reads these marks and subsequently makes the proper analyses necessary to produce a written report.

Figure 5 depicts a sample, computerized, mental status *report* which could be produced from the input forms as shown in Figure 4. Since all possible words, phrases, and statements have been previously programmed into a computer report "dictionary," virtually any combination of these items can be printed out. In fact, thousands of words, phrases, and statements may have to be

MENTAL STATUS EXAMINATION   PAGE 1 OF 4

INSTRUCTIONS: FILL IN ONLY THOSE ITEMS WHICH ARE OF POSITIVE <u>OR</u> NEGATIVE IMPORTANCE.

PATIENT IDENTIFICATION NUMBER

:0: :1: :2:

:0: :1: :2: :3: :4:   :5: :6: :7: :8: :9:
:0: :1: :2: :3: :4:   :5: :6: :7: :8: :9:
:0: :1: :2: :3: :4:   :5: :6: :7: :8: :9:
:0: :1: :2: :3: :4:   :5: :6: :7: :8: :9:
:0: :1: :2: :3: :4:   :5: :6: :7: :8: :9:
:0: :1: :2: :3: :4:   :5: :6: :7: :8: :9:

DOCTOR NUMBER

:0: :1: :2: :3: :4:   :5: :6: :7: :8: :9:
:0: :1: :2: :3: :4:   :5: :6: :7: :8: :9:
:0: :1: :2: :3: :4:   :5: :6: :7: :8: :9:

DATE

:0: :1: :2: :3:
:0: :1: :2: :3: :4:   :5: :6: :7: :8: :9:

JAN FEB MAR APR MAY   JUN JUL AUG SEP OCT
NOV DEC :66: :67: :68:   :69: :70: :71: :72: :73:

HOSPITAL NUMBER

:0: :1: :2: :3: :4:   :5: :6: :7: :8: :9:
:0: :1: :2: :3: :4:   :5: :6: :7: :8: :9:

SEX OF THE PATIENT   MALE   FEMALE

PATIENT'S AGE

:0: :1: :2: :3: :4:   :5: :6: :7: :8: :9:
:0: :1: :2: :3: :4:   :5: :6: :7: :8: :9:

THE PATIENT LOOKS   HIS AGE   OLDER   YOUNGER

APPARENT PHYSICAL HEALTH   NORMAL   FAIR   POOR   EXCELLENT

COMMUNICATION BARRIERS   DEGREE OF INTERFERENCE

	NONE	MILDLY	MODERATELY	MARKEDLY
DEAFNESS				
BLINDNESS				
MUTISM				
AN ATTENTION DEFICIT				
OTHER RESPONSE DEFICIT				

SPECIFY ______________________________

PATIENT ______________________________

DOCTOR ______________________________

DATE ______________ HOSPITAL __________

PREDOMINANT FEATURES IN BODY BUILD ARE:
     UNREMARKABLE ::
MESOMORPHIC :::::   ENDOMORPHIC :::::   ECTOMORPHIC ::

PHYSICAL DEFORMITY   NONE   MILD   MODERATE   MARKED

DRESS:
   UNREMARKABLE :::::   METICULOUS ::
   UNTIDY :::::   ATTENTION SEEKING :::::   INSTITUTIONAL
   DIRTY :::::   BIZARRE :::::   NOT APPROPRIATE TO THE OCCASSION

FACIAL EXPRESSION
   UNREMARKABLE ::::: IMMOBILE ::::: ANXIOUS
SAD :::::   TEARFUL ::::: FRIGHTENED ::::: PERPLEXED
ELATED :::::   ECSTATIC ::::: HOSTILE ::::: GRIMACING ::

POSTURE

	UNREMARKABLE	SLIGHTLY	MODERATELY	MARKED
STOOPED				
STIFF				
BIZARRE				
OTHER				
SUGGESTIVE OF NEUROLOGICAL DISORDER				

GAIT

	UNREMARKABLE	SLIGHTLY	MODERATELY	MARKED
UNSTEADY				
RIGID				
SHUFFLING				
MANNERISTIC				
STEREOTYPED				
SUGGESTIVE OF NEUROLOGICAL DISORDER				

FIGURE 4A. MENTAL STATUS EXAMINATION.

Courtesy of Kline, N. S., and Laska, E., Rockland State Hospital, Orangeburg, New York. Appeared originally in their book, *Computers and Electronic Devices in Psychiatry.* New York, Grune & Stratton, 1968.

<u>**MENTAL STATUS EXAMINATION**</u>   <u>**PAGE 2 OF 4**</u>

OTHER BODY MOVEMENTS

UNREMARKABLE	SLIGHTLY	MODERATELY	MARKEDLY
TREMOR			
TICS			
MANNERISMS			
STEREOTYPED			
GENERALIZED MOTOR DISTURBANCE SUGGESTIVE HYSTERICAL REACTION			

GENERAL BEHAVIOR AND ACTIVITY

UNREMARKABLE	SLIGHTLY	MODERATELY	MARKEDLY
HISTRIONIC			
NEGATIVISTIC			
AGGRESSIVE			
IMPULSIVE			
ALLO-EROTIC			
AUTO-EROTIC			
AUTOMATICALLY OBEDIENT			
OBSESSIONAL			
ECHOPRAXIC			
DESTRUCTIVE			
DEPENDENT			
PASSIVE			
WITHDRAWN			
UNCOOPERATIVE			

ABNORMAL BEHAVIOR DIRECTED TOWARD

	SELF	OBJECTS	OTHERS

AFFECT

NORMAL	SLIGHTLY	MODERATELY	MARKEDLY
ANXIOUS			
PERPLEXED			
HOSTILE			
FRIGHTENED			
DEPRESSED			
EUPHORIC			

AFFECT (cont'd)

INCONGRUOUS	SLIGHTLY	MODERATELY	MARKEDLY
FLATTENED			
EXCITED			
PESSIMISM ABOUT THE FUTURE			
SELF-REPROACH			
NARROWED INTERESTS			
INDECISION			
FEELINGS OF GUILT			
SUICIDAL PRE-OCCUPATIONS			

BIOLOGICAL-VEGETATIVE

CYCLOTHYMIA	NONE	MILD	MODERATE	MARKED
DIURNAL VARIATION: MORNING				
EVENING				
SLEEP DISTURBANCE: EARLY PHASE				
MIDDLE PHASE				
LATE PHASE				
DURING DAY				
LOSS OF APPETITE				
LOSS OF ENERGY				
LOSS OF WEIGHT				
SEXUAL FUNCTIONING (HYPERACTIVITY)	NORMAL			
(HYPOACTIVITY)				

SELF CONCERN—PSYCHOPHYSIOLOGICAL

CONCERN WITH HEALTH	NONE	MILD	MODERATE	MARKED

	MILD	MODERATE	MARKED
HEADACHE			
SKIN DISORDER			
MUSCULO-SKELETAL DISORDER			
RESPIRATORY DISORDER			
CARDIOVASCULAR			
GASTRO-INTESTINAL			
GENITO-URINARY			

FIGURE 4B. MENTAL STATUS EXAMINATION.

MENTAL STATUS EXAMINATION   PAGE 3 OF 4

SELF CONCERN–PSYCHOPHYSIOLOGICAL (CONT'D)

SUGGESTING HYSTERIA	MILD	MODERATE	MARKED
ANESTHESIA			
HYPERASTHESIA			
BLINDNESS			
DEAFNESS			
PARALYSIS			
IMPOTENCE			
FRIGIDITY			

	NONE	MILD	MODERATE	MARKED
HYPOCHONDRIASIS				

SPEECH

	MILD	MODERATE	MARKED
SHOUTING			
SCREAMING			
PERSEVERATION			
CIRCUMSTANTIALITY			
TALKING PAST THE POINT			
ACCELERATION			
RETARDATION			
FLIGHT OF IDEAS			
DISJOINTED SPEECH			

CONTENT OF SPEECH INCLUDED:

SLANG ASSOCIATIONS   CURSING   UNINTELLIGIBLE MUTTERINGS

VERBAL STEREOTYPES   NEOLOGISMS   ECHOALIA

	ABSENT	MILD	MODERATE	MARKED
POVERTY OF SPEECH				

PERCEPTION

	MILD	MODERATE	MARKED
NORMAL			
ILLUSIONS			
HALLUCINATIONS			

	HYPNAGOGIC STATE	WAKING STATE	BOTH
OCCURRING IN THE			

CONTENT:

SELF-DEROGATORY	
THREATENING	ACCUSATORY
GRANDIOSE	RELIGIOSE
SEXUAL	MAGICAL
FLATTERING	RUNNING COMMENTARIES

PATIENT ______________________

PERCEPTION (CONT'D)

MODALITY		
	AUDITORY	
VISUAL	OLFACTORY	
GUSTATORY	TACTILE	

PERCEPTUO-COGNITIVE-BODY IMAGE

	NORMAL	MILD	MODERATE	MARKED
NORMAL				
DEREALIZATION				
DEPERSONALIZATION				
DETEMPORALIZATION				
DEJA VU				
JAMAIS VU				
SPECIFIC BODY IMAGE DISTURBANCE				
OTHER				

COGNITION
THOUGHT PROCESS

	NORMAL	MILD	MODERATE	MARKED
NORMAL				
ACCELERATION				
RETARDATION				
OBSESSIVE–RUMINATIVE				
BLOCKING				
DISORDERED CONCEPTUALIZATION				
DISORGANIZATION				
LOOSE ASSOCIATIONS				

CONTENT INCLUDED

	MILD	MODERATE	MARKED
PERSECUTORY DELUSIONS			
PASSIVITY EXPERIENCES			
HYPOCHONDRIACAL DELUSIONS			
NIHILISTIC DELUSIONS			
GRANDIOSE DELUSIONS			
RELIGIOSE DELUSIONS			
DELUSIONS OF SPOUSE INFIDELITY			
SEXUAL DELUSIONS			
SELF DEROGATORY DELUSIONS			

FIGURE 4C. MENTAL STATUS EXAMINATION.

MENTAL STATUS EXAMINATION

PATIENT IDENTIFICATION NUMBER

0	1	2	3	4	5	6	7	8	9
0	1	2	3	4	5	6	7	8	9
0	1	2	3	4	5	6	7	8	9
0	1	2	3	4	5	6	7	8	9
0	1	2	3	4	5	6	7	8	9
0	1	2	3	4	5	6	7	8	9
0	1	2	3	4	5	6	7	8	9

COGNITION (CONT'D)

	MILD	MODERATE	MARKED
DELUSIONS OF GUILT	⋯	⋯	⋯

SPECIFY CONTENT ________________________

	MILD	MODERATE	MARKED
IDEAS OF REFERENCE	⋯	⋯	⋯

SPECIFY CONTENT ________________________

	MILD	MODERATE	MARKED
PHOBIAS	⋯	⋯	⋯

SPECIFY CONTENT ________________________

SENSORIUM

	MILD	MODERATE	MARKED
CLEAR	⋯		
CLOUDING OF CONSCIOUSNESS	⋯	⋯	⋯
FLUCTUANT	⋯	⋯	⋯
CONTINUOUS	⋯	⋯	⋯
EPISODIC	⋯	⋯	⋯

ORIENTATION

NORMAL ⋯   NOT TESTABLE ⋯

DISORIENTATION	MILD	MODERATE	MARKED
FOR TIME	⋯	⋯	⋯
FOR PLACE	⋯	⋯	⋯
FOR PERSON	⋯	⋯	⋯

ATTENTION

	ADEQUATE	MILDLY IMPAIRED	MODERATELY IMPAIRED	MARKEDLY IMPAIRED
ATTENTION/CONCENTRATION	⋯	⋯	⋯	⋯
ABSTRACT REASONING	⋯	⋯	⋯	⋯

MEMORY

	NORMAL	MILDLY IMPAIRED	MODERATELY IMPAIRED	MARKEDLY IMPAIRED
NOT TESTABLE	⋯	⋯	⋯	⋯

	MILD	MODERATE	MARKED
CIRCUMSCRIBED IMPAIRMENT FOR RECENT EVENTS	⋯	⋯	⋯
CIRCUMSCRIBED IMPAIRMENT FOR REMOTE EVENTS	⋯	⋯	⋯
GENERAL IMPAIRMENT FOR RECENT EVENTS	⋯	⋯	⋯
GENERAL IMPAIRMENT FOR REMOTE EVENTS	⋯	⋯	⋯

INTELLIGENCE

NOT TESTABLE ⋯   AVERAGE ⋯   ABOVE AVERAGE ⋯

BELOW AVERAGE ⋯   SUBNORMAL ⋯   SEVERELY SUBNORMAL ⋯

	NO LACK	MILD LACK	MODERATE LACK	MARKED LACK
INSIGHT	⋯	⋯	⋯	⋯

	NORMAL	MILDLY	MODERATELY	MARKEDLY
JUDGEMENT	⋯	⋯	⋯	⋯

– IMPAIRED –

SELF APPRAISAL

ADEQUATE ⋯

	MILDLY	MODERATELY	MARKEDLY
TIMID	⋯	⋯	⋯
GRANDIOSE	⋯	⋯	⋯
UNREALISTIC	⋯	⋯	⋯
INFERIORITY FEELING	⋯	⋯	⋯
INADEQUACY FEELING	⋯	⋯	⋯

RESPONSIBILITY

	NORMAL	MILD LACK	MODERATE LACK	MARKED LACK
SOCIAL AREA	⋯	⋯	⋯	⋯
FAMILY CIRCLE	⋯	⋯	⋯	⋯
FINANCIAL AREAS	⋯	⋯	⋯	⋯
EMPLOYMENT AREAS	⋯	⋯	⋯	⋯

SEXUAL MALADAPTATION

NORMAL ⋯

	MILD	MODERATE	MARKED
SEXUAL ASSAULT	⋯	⋯	⋯
SADISM	⋯	⋯	⋯
MASOCHISM	⋯	⋯	⋯
FETISHISM	⋯	⋯	⋯
TRANSVESTISM	⋯	⋯	⋯
VOYEURISM	⋯	⋯	⋯
MUTILATION	⋯	⋯	⋯
PROMISCUITY	⋯	⋯	⋯
HOMOSEXUALITY	⋯	⋯	⋯

DIFFERENTIAL DIAGNOSIS ________________________

____

____

____

FIGURE 4D. MENTAL STATUS EXAMINATION.

stored in the computer's memory in order to handle many different narrative configurations.

The computerized report can be as personalized and as tailor-made for the patient as a manually-written one can be. But, the computer must be programmed with a large dictionary or vocabulary if report individuality is to be achieved. Furthermore, the input code sheets must be designed so as to provide diversification and flexibility of input reporting needs.

Note that the sample report in Figure 5 is slightly different from a report that one would have written manually on "patient no. 197." In the first place the computer which was used to write this report was programmed to print out all alternatives for the patient's mental status. Negative statements were included such as "There is *no* evidence of cyclothymia. There is *no* disturbance of sleep pattern." Also, no diagnosis or recommendations for treatment were indicated. On the positive side, one can very well program a computer to write a report style suited to any specific needs.

A much more comprehensive computer report is illustrated in Figure 6. Hence, the relevant demographic, physical, emotional, social, diagnostic, and treatment follow-up data are indicated. A report such as this could function as a psychiatric evaluation, progress note, predischarge evaluation, or the like. This report is *action-oriented*, meaning that the clinician has a more concrete base from which to plan the patient's treatment program. The material included in each of these two reports results from a) specific input data the clinician sent to the computer, and b) the nature of the computer program. Each type of report was designed to serve a specific purpose.

A report which could be very effectively used by the social or case worker is the *developmental history*. Information relating to the patient's overall past involvements can be included on a form such as this. Family structure and relationships, family attitudes, the patient's physical, social, and emotional development from childhood, and pre-morbid and present status can be recorded in the developmental history. A history report would be an important supportive measure to the mental status report. Both reports could be used to generate a computer input in order

FIGURE 5. MENTAL STATUS REPORT.

Courtesy of IBM Corporation, White Plains, New York. From their Technical Manual E20-0291, *Clinical and Administrative Record System: Information Processing for the Mental Hospital*, p. 21.

Patient no. 197

Examining Doctor no.

Hospital no. 17

Date of examination September 14, 1966

The patient is a male who looks older than his age, appears to be in normal physical health, and is unremarkable in body build. He has no physical deformity. The patient is troubled with a nonspecific response defect that interferes moderately with communication. The facial expression of the patient in unremarkable and his dress is institutional. His posture is slightly stooped. However, his gait is unremarkable. Other body movements are unremarkable.

His general behavior is slightly aggressive and mainly directed towards others.

The affect is one of slight hostility and moderate flattening. There is associated marked narrowness of interests and moderate indecision.

There is no evidence of cyclothymia. There is no disturbance of sleep pattern. There is no loss of appetite, no loss of energy, and no loss of weight. The patient has no complaints of disturbance in sexual activity.

He is not concerned with current health.

His speech shows mild tendency to disjointed speech. Speech content includes neologisms. There is mild blocking, moderate disordered conceptualization, moderate disorganization, and marked loose associations apparent in the thought process.

Perception is disturbed to a mild degree by hallucinations which occurred in the waking state in the auditory modality with self-derogatory content.

Sensorium is clear.

There is moderate disorientation for time and there is moderate disorientation for place.

Attention-concentration is adequate. There is a marked defect in abstract reasoning and memory shows moderate general impairment for recent events and moderate general impairment for remote events. Intelligence of the patient is not testable and his insight is considered to be markedly lacking. The patient has mild inferiority feelings.

The patient shows no evidence of sexual maladaptation.

134   *Writing Psychological Reports*

Figure 6. System Progress Note.

Courtesy of IBM Corporation, White Plains, New York. From their Technical Manual E20-0291, *Clinical and Administrative Record System: Information Processing for the Mental Hospital*, p. 28.

Patient Name	Hospital Name and Number	Note Date
		01/26/66

ID Number	Consec. No.	Age	Sex	Ethnic Group	Marital	Legal
1002896	070095	78	male	white	married	2 pc.

Adm. Date
10/05/65

Diagnosis: Psychosis with syphilitic meningo-encephalitis.

General health: Bed patient, serious somatic problem, underweight, no weight change, poor eating habits.

Physical appearance: Decreased motor activity, neat.

Activities: None at all.

Insight to illness: Lacking.

General judgment. Lacking.

Emotional reaction: Affect is inappropriate, depressed.

Attitude and general behavior: Never or infrequently is incontinent, ingratiating, sociable. Frequently is cooperative, withdrawn, irritable, hostile and aggressive, behavior conforms to group. Good adjustment to hospitalization. Poor future planning, attitude toward family relationship.

Sensorium: Orientation to time, place, person. Recent memory is markedly impaired. Remote memory is markedly impaired. Abstract thinking is markedly impaired. Intellectual ability is normal.

Subsequent course. No change.

Stream of mental activity. Rambling, irrelevant, confused. Below average verbal productivity.

Thought content: No hallucinations. No delusions. No neurotic symptoms.

Privileges: Visitors, open ward.

Psychotropic medication: Maintain same dosage of tranquilizer.

---

to produce a comprehensive psychological report on the client. Figure 7 shows a sample Developmental History form for use with an optical scanning device.

A multipurpose answer sheet for use with optical scanning devices is shown in Figure 8. This 240-item form is very appropriate for either a True-False or a multiple-choice response model. Almost any type of data could be recorded on a form of

DEVELOPMENTAL HISTORY

INSTRUCTIONS: FILL IN ONLY THOSE ITEMS WHICH ARE OF POSITIVE OR NEGATIVE IMPORTANCE.

PATIENT IDENTIFICATION NUMBER

1	2	3	4	5	6	7	8	9
1	2	3	4	5	6	7	8	9
1	2	3	4	5	6	7	8	9
1	2	3	4	5	6	7	8	9
1	2	3	4	5	6	7	8	9
1	2	3	4	5	6	7	8	9
1	2	3	4	5	6	7	8	9

DOCTOR'S NUMBER

1	2	3	4	5	6	7	8	9
1	2	3	4	5	6	7	8	9
1	2	3	4	5	6	7	8	9

DATE

1	2	3						
1	2	3	4	5	6	7	8	9

JAN	FEB	MAR	APR	MAY	JUN	JUL	AUG	SEP	OCT
NOV	DEC	'66	'67	'68	'69	'70	'71	'72	'73

HOSPITAL NUMBER

1	2	3	4	5	6	7	8	9
1	2	3	4	5	6	7	8	9

SOURCES OF INFORMATION-CONTRIBUTIONS

	NOT A SOURCE	ONLY SOURCE	MINOR SOURCE	IMPORTANT SOURCE	MAJOR SOURCE
PATIENT					
FATHER					
MOTHER					
SPOUSE					
BROTHER					
SISTER					
ANOTHER FAMILY MEMBER (SPECIFY)					
ANOTHER PERSON (SPECIFY)					

SIGNIFICANT FACTORS IN PREGNANCY

	BY MUTUAL AGREEMENT	ON MOTHER INITIATIVE	ON FATHER INITIATIVE
BIRTH: NEONATAL SITUATION			
ADOPTED AS A BABY			

ATTITUDE OF PARENTS TO PREGNANCY	BY BOTH	BY MOTHER ONLY	BY FATHER ONLY
PLANNED			
WANTED			
UNPLANNED			
UNWANTED			
CHILD OF OPPOSITE SEX PREFERRED			
AMBIVALENT ATTITUDES			

PATIENT'S NAME

DOCTOR'S NAME

DATE ___________ HOSPITAL ___________

	MALE	FEMALE
SEX OF THE PATIENT		

PATIENT'S AGE (ESTIMATE IF UNKNOWN)

0	1	2	3	4	5	6	7	8	9

MATERNAL AGE AT DELIVERY

0	1	2	3	4	5	6	7	8	9
0	1	2	3	4	5	6	7	8	9

MATERNAL HEALTH IN PREGNANCY

EXCELLENT

UPSET BY NAUSEA OR VOMITING — IN EARLY STAGES — IN LATE STAGES

PRE ECLAMPTIC TOXEMIA — ECLAMPSIA

OTHER PHYSICAL ILLNESS OR OBSTETRIC COMPLICATION — SPECIFY ___________

DRUG USAGE IN PREGNANCY BY MOTHER

ADDICTIVE DRUG — EARLY STAGES — LATE STAGES — THROUGHOUT — SPECIFY ___________

NON-ADDICTIVE DRUG — EARLY STAGES — LATE STAGES — THROUGHOUT — SPECIFY ___________

PERI-NATAL PERIOD

DELIVERY WAS	ON TIME	PRE MATURE	POST MATURE	NORMAL	INSTRU-MENTAL	CAESAR-EAN

COMPLICATIONS

DELAY IN LABOR	BREECH OR ABNORMAL PRESENTATION	PLACENTA PRAEVIA OR ACCIDENTAL BLEEDING

CONDITION AT BIRTH	NORMAL	JAUNDICED
ANOXIC	REQUIRED TRANSFUSION	REQUIRED INCUBATOR
HAD PARALYSIS	REQUIRED RESUSCITATION	HAD A HEAD DEFORMITY

INFANCY

WEANING	NORMAL	EARLY	LATE	
	NO PROBLEM	SOME PROBLEM	SERIOUS PROBLEM	MOTHER OBJECTED TO METHOD
FORMULA FED				
BREAST FED				

PHYSICAL DEVELOPMENT

	NORMAL	ACCEL-ERATED	SLOW	RETARDED	CAUSED PARENTAL CONCERN		INDUCED PARENTS TO SEEK MEDICAL ADVICE WHICH WAS	
					YES	NO	NEEDED	NOT NEEDED
GROWTH								
MOTOR ACTIVITY								
SPEECH								
COORDINATION								

INFANCY (TO AGE 5)

	ONCE	TWICE	THREE TIMES	FOUR OR MORE TIMES
INFANT REQUIRED HOSPITALIZATION				

TOTAL PERIOD IN MONTHS

1	2	3	4	5	6	7	8	9
0	1	2	3	4	5	6	7	8	9

SPECIFY REASONS ___________

	LITTLE OR NONE	MILDLY	MODER-ATELY	MARK-EDLY
HOSPITALIZATION THOUGHT TO INTERFERE WITH ADJUSTMENT AND PROGRESS				

FIGURE 7A. DEVELOPMENTAL HISTORY.

Courtesy of Kline, N. S., and Laska, E., Rockland State Hospital, Orangeburg, New York. Appeared originally in their book, *Computers and Electronic Devices in Psychiatry.* New York, Grune & Stratton, 1968.

PSYCHIC DEVELOPMENT

BABY WAS DESCRIBED AS: NORMAL :::::

UNUSUALLY GOOD   :::::   GIVEN TO FREQUENT CRYING   :::::

GIVEN TO TEMPER TANTRUMS :::::   GIVEN TO HEAD BANGING   :::::

GIVEN TO NIGHT TERRORS :::::   GIVEN TO UNREASONABLE FEARS :::::

GIVEN TO COLDS OR OTHER UPPER   GIVEN TO FOOD FADS OR
RESPIRATORY INFECTIONS   :::::   CHOOSY ABOUT FEEDING   :::::

	NOT AT ALL	MILDLY	MODER- ATELY	MARK- EDLY
NERVOUS	:::::	:::::	:::::	:::::

BABY EXHIBITED: SLEEPWALKING ::::: FEAR OF THE DARK   :::::

NAIL BITING :::::   OVERACTIVITY ::::: TEETH GRINDING   :::::

TICS   :::::   OTHER   ::::: SPECIFY ________________

	FAST	NORMAL	SLOW	WITH REGRESSIONS
BLADDER CONTROL DEVELOPED	:::::	:::::	:::::	:::::
BOWEL CONTROL DEVELOPED	:::::	:::::	:::::	:::::

	INDUL- GENT	PERMIS- SIVE	RIGID	PUNI- TIVE
MATERNAL ATTITUDE TO TOILET TRAINING	:::::	:::::	:::::	:::::

PSYCHOLOGICAL UPSET
MAY HAVE RESULTED FROM

AN ASSAULT :::::   *MATERNAL DEPRIVATION :::::   AN ACCIDENT :::::
(SEXUAL)

AN- ASSAULT :::::   *PATERNAL DEPRIVATION :::::   *OTHER   :::::
(NON-SEXUAL)

*SPECIFY WHAT IS MEANT ________________________

AGE FORMAL SCHOOLING BEGAN

:0:: ::1:: :2:: :3::

:0:: ::1:: :2:: :3:: :4::   :5:: :6:: :7:: :8:: :9::

AGE FORMAL SCHOOLING ENDED

:0:: ::1:: :2:: :3:: :4::   :5:: :6::

:0:: ::1:: :2:: :3:: :4::   :5:: :6:: :7:: :8:: :9::

FORMAL SCHOOLING

NURSERY SCHOOL:

	POOR	AVERAGE	GOOD	EXCELLENT
PROGRESS	:::::	:::::	:::::	:::::
RELATIONS WITH PEERS	:::::	:::::	:::::	:::::
RELATIONS WITH TEACHERS	:::::	:::::	:::::	:::::

KINDERGARTEN

PROGRESS	:::::	:::::	:::::	:::::
RELATIONS WITH PEERS	:::::	:::::	:::::	:::::
RELATIONS WITH TEACHERS	:::::	:::::	:::::	:::::

GRADE SCHOOL

PROGRESS	:::::	:::::	:::::	:::::
RELATIONS WITH PEERS	:::::	:::::	:::::	:::::
RELATIONS WITH TEACHERS	:::::	:::::	:::::	:::::

HIGH SCHOOL

PROGRESS	:::::	:::::	:::::	:::::
RELATIONS WITH PEERS	:::::	:::::	:::::	:::::
RELATIONS WITH TEACHERS	:::::	:::::	:::::	:::::

COLLEGE

PROGRESS	:::::	:::::	:::::	:::::
RELATIONS WITH PEERS	:::::	:::::	:::::	:::::
RELATIONS WITH TEACHERS	:::::	:::::	:::::	:::::

POST GRADUATE SCHOOL

PROGRESS	:::::	:::::	:::::	:::::
RELATIONS WITH PEERS	:::::	:::::	:::::	:::::
RELATIONS WITH TEACHERS	:::::	:::::	:::::	:::::

	DEFIC- IENT LOW	ADEQU- ATE REAL- ISTIC	IN EXCESS OF NEEDS HIGH	UNSUIT- ABLE EXCES- SIVE
PATIENT ASSESSES EDUCATION AS:	:::::	:::::	:::::	:::::
PARENTAL DEMAND ON EDUCATIONAL PROGRESS	:::::	:::::	:::::	:::::

PATIENT WAS ABLE TO COMPLY WITH DEMANDS?   YES NO

SOCIAL ADAPTATION

	HIGHLY COMPETITIVE	AN ADEQUATE PARTICIPATOR	AN INTERESTED OBSERVER	TO[TAL] LA[TE] INT[E]
IN SPORTS	:::::	:::::	:::::	
IN SOCIAL ACTIVITIES	:::::	:::::	:::::	
IN HOBBIES OR SPECIAL INTERESTS	:::::	:::::	:::::	

SOCIO-SEXUAL DEVELOPMENT

	FATHER MOTHER	SIBLING OTHER RELATIVE	PEERS SELF ACQUIRED	INSTRUC[TOR] O[THER] SO[URCE]	SCH[OOL]
SOURCE OF SEX EDUCATION WAS MAINLY	::::: :::::	::::: :::::	::::: :::::		

PATIENT VIEWS SEX EDUCATION AS

	ADEQUATE	TOO VAGUE	TOO LITTLE	B[A] P[] SE[]
IN INFANCY	:::::	:::::	:::::	
IN PRE-ADOLESCENCE	:::::	:::::	:::::	
IN ADOLESCENCE	:::::	:::::	:::::	
AS AN ADULT	:::::	:::::	:::::	

	ADE- QUATE NORMAL	DEFIC- IENT EARLY	INAPP[] PRI[] L[]
FEELS THAT CURRENT KNOWLEDGE FOR STAGE OF LIFE IS	:::::	:::::	
PUBERTY ATTAINED	AGE	:::::	

SPECIFY AGE

:0:: ::1:: :2::

:0:: ::1:: :2:: :3:: :4::   :5:: :6:: :7:: :8:: ::

	ADEQUATE	MILDLY DEFICIENT	MODERATELY DEFICIENT	MARK[EDLY] DEFICI[ENT]
PATIENT FEELS THAT PREPARATION FOR PUBERTY WAS:	:::::	:::::	:::::	

SEXUAL EXPERIENCE

INFANCY TO AGE 5

	DENIED	RARE	OCCA- SIONAL	FRE- QUENT	
AUTOEROTIC PRACTICES WERE:	:::::	:::::	:::::	:::::	

	HETERO SEXUAL	HOMO SEXUAL	MASO- CHISTIC	SAD- ISTIC	NO[] SEX[]
ASSOCIATED FANTASIES MAINLY	:::::	:::::	:::::	:::::	

VAGINAL COITUS :::::

	HETERO- SEXUAL	HOMO SEXUAL	BO[]
PETTING	:::::	:::::	
MASTURBATION	:::::	:::::	
ORAL-GENITAL	:::::	:::::	:::
ANAL COITUS	:::::	:::::	:::
GROUP ACTIVITY	:::::	:::::	:::

PRE-ADOLESCENCE

	DENIED	RARE	OCCA- SIONAL	FRE- QUENT	
AUTOEROTIC PRACTICES WERE:	:::::	:::::	:::::	:::::	

	HETERO SEXUAL	HOMO SEXUAL	MASO- CHRISTIC	SAD- ISTIC	NO[] SEXU[]
ASSOCIATED FANTASIES MAINLY	:::::	:::::	:::::	:::::	

VAGINAL COITUS :::::

	HETERO- SEXUAL	HOMO SEXUAL	BO[]
PETTING	:::::	:::::	:::
MASTURBATION	:::::	:::::	:::
ORAL-GENITAL	:::::	:::::	:::
ANAL COITUS	:::::	:::::	:::
GROUP ACTIVITY	:::::	:::::	:::

FIGURE 7B. DEVELOPMENTAL HISTORY.

DEVELOPMENTAL HISTORY

SEXUAL EXPERIENCE (CONTINUED)

ADOLESCENCE

AUTOEROTIC PRACTICES WERE: DENIED · RARE · OCCASIONAL · FREQUENT

ASSOCIATED FANTASIES MAINLY: HETEROSEXUAL · HOMOSEXUAL · MASOCHISTIC · SADISTIC · NON-SEXUAL

VAGINAL COITUS

                  HETEROSEXUAL · HOMOSEXUAL · BOTH

    PETTING

    MASTURBATION

    ORAL-GENITAL

    ANAL COITUS

    GROUP ACTIVITY

PRE-MARITALLY

AUTOEROTIC PRACTICES WERE: DENIED · RARE · OCCASIONAL · FREQUENT

ASSOCIATED FANTASIES MAINLY: HETEROSEXUAL · HOMOSEXUAL · MASOCHISTIC · SADISTIC · NON-SEXUAL

VAGINAL COITUS

                  HETEROSEXUAL · HOMOSEXUAL · BOTH

    PETTING

    MASTURBATION

    ORAL-GENITAL

    ANAL COITUS

    GROUP ACTIVITY

MARITALLY

AUTOEROTIC PRACTICES WERE: DENIED · RARE · OCCASIONAL · FREQUENT

ASSOCIATED FANTASIES MAINLY: HETEROSEXUAL · HOMOSEXUAL · MASOCHISTIC · SADISTIC · NON-SEXUAL

VAGINAL COITUS

                  HETEROSEXUAL · HOMOSEXUAL · BOTH

    PETTING

    MASTURBATION

    ORAL-GENITAL

    ANAL COITUS

    GROUP ACTIVITY

EXTRA MARITALLY

    VAGINAL COITUS

                  HETEROSEXUAL · HOMOSEXUAL · BOTH

    PETTING

    MASTURBATION

    ORAL-GENITAL

    ANAL COITUS

    GROUP ACTIVITY

SEXUAL ATTITUDES AND ADJUSTMENT

DOES PATIENT REGARD HIS SEXUAL BEHAVIOR AS PROMISCUOUS? YES · NO

DOES INTERVIEWER AGREE WITH PATIENT'S OPINION? YES · NO

DOES PATIENT CONSIDER HIS PAST BEHAVIOR ABNORMAL? YES · NO

WAS IT ACCEPTED BY HIS SEXUAL PARTNER(S)? YES · NO

WAS IT A CAUSE OF:

FAMILY PROBLEMS YES · NO   MARITAL DISHARMONY YES · NO

SOCIAL DISHARMONY YES · NO   OCCUPATIONAL DISHARMONY YES · NO

TROUBLE WITH THE LAW YES · NO   RELIGIOUS CONFLICT YES · NO

PATIENT'S NAME ______________________________

DOES PATIENT CONSIDER HIS PRESENT BEHAVIOR ABNORMAL? YES · NO

IS IT ACCEPTED BY HIS SEXUAL PARTNER(S)? YES · NO

IS IT A CAUSE OF:

FAMILY PROBLEMS YES · NO   MARITAL DISHARMONY YES · NO

SOCIAL DISHARMONY YES · NO   OCCUPATIONAL DISHARMONY YES · NO

TROUBLE WITH THE LAW YES · NO   RELIGIOUS CONFLICT YES · NO

COURTSHIP AND MARITAL PATTERN

HOW MANY TIMES HAS THE PATIENT BEEN MARRIED? 0 · 1 · 2 · 3 · 4 · 5 · 6 · 7 · 8 · 9

SPECIFY MARRIAGE BEING DESCRIBED 1 · 2 · 3 · 4 · 5 · 6 · 7 · 8 · 9

AGE AT MARRIAGE 1 · 2 · 3 · 4 · 5 · 6 · 7 · 8 · 9

0 · 1 · 2 · 3 · 4 · 5 · 6 · 7 · 8 · 9

KNEW SPOUSE — LESS THAN 6 MONTHS · 6 MONTHS-1 YEAR · 2+ YEARS

COURTSHIP LASTED

COURSE OF COURTSHIP — UNBROKEN · OCCASIONAL BREAKUP · FREQUENT BREAKUP · MANY BREAKUPS

DECISION TO MARRY — BY MUTUAL FREE CONSENT

    PREGNANCY   PARENTAL PRESSURE   OTHER PRESSURE

SPECIFY ______________________________

ENTHUSIASTIC ACCEPTANCE OF MARRIAGE BY:

    PATIENT ONLY   SPOUSE ONLY   BOTH   NEITHER

    PATIENT'S FAMILY   SPOUSE'S FAMILY   BOTH   NEITHER

MARRIAGE RESENTED BY:

    PATIENT ONLY   SPOUSE ONLY   BOTH

    PATIENT'S FAMILY   SPOUSE'S FAMILY   BOTH

CURRENT STATUS OF MARRIAGE

    VERGE OF BREAK-UP   DESERTION OF — PATIENT · SPOUSE

BROKEN UP BY: MUTUAL SEPARATION

    DIVORCE OR ANNULMENT   DEATH OF SPOUSE

FIGURE 7C. DEVELOPMENTAL HISTORY.

DEVELOPMENTAL HISTORY

PATIENT IDENTIFICATION NUMBER

0	1	2	3	4	5	6	7	8	9
0	1	2	3	4	5	6	7	8	9
0	1	2	3	4	5	6	7	8	9
0	1	2	3	4	5	6	7	8	9
0	1	2	3	4	5	6	7	8	9
0	1	2	3	4	5	6	7	8	9
0	1	2	3	4	5	6	7	8	9

IF PATIENT HAS BEEN MARRIED MORE THAN ONE TIME AND ANOTHER MARRIAGE IS DESCRIBED, FILL OUT THE SECTION BELOW. OTHERWISE SKIP THIS SECTION AND CONTINUE AT THE TOP OF THE NEXT COLUMN.

COURTSHIP AND MARITAL PATTERN (CONT'D)
SPECIFY MARRIAGE BEING DESCRIBED

1	2	3	4	5	6	7	8	9

AGE AT MARRIAGE

1	2	3	4	5	6	7	8	9
0	1	2	3	4	5	6	7	8	9

COURTSHIP

	LESS THAN 6 MONTHS	6 MONTHS TO 1 YEAR	2+ YEARS
KNEW SPOUSE			
COURTSHIP LASTED	⋯	⋯	⋯

	UN-BROKEN	OCCASIONAL BREAKUP	FREQUENT BREAKUP	MANY BREAKUPS
COURSE OF COURTSHIP	⋯	⋯	⋯	⋯

DECISION TO MARRY

BY MUTUAL FREE CONSENT ⋯

PREGNANCY ⋯   PARENTAL PRESSURE ⋯   OTHER PRESSURE ⋯

SPECIFY ________________________

ENTHUSIASTIC ACCEPTANCE OF MARRIAGE BY:

PATIENT ONLY ⋯   SPOUSE ONLY ⋯   BOTH ⋯   NEITHER ⋯

PATIENT'S FAMILY ⋯   SPOUSE'S FAMILY ⋯   BOTH ⋯   NEITHER ⋯

MARRIAGE RESENTED BY:

PATIENT ONLY ⋯   SPOUSE ONLY ⋯   BOTH ⋯

PATIENT'S FAMILY ⋯   SPOUSE'S FAMILY ⋯   BOTH ⋯

CURRENT STATUS OF MARRIAGE :

BROKEN UP BY: VERGE OF BREAK-UP ⋯

DESERTION OF: PATIENT ⋯   SPOUSE ⋯

MUTUAL SEPARATION ⋯   DEATH OF SPOUSE ⋯

DIVORCE OR ANNULMENT ⋯

PRE-MORBID PERSONALITY

SELECT ADJECTIVES WHICH WOULD APPEAR MOST APPROPRIATE TO DESCRIBING THE PATIENT BEFORE ILLNESS AND GRADE THE EXTENT TO WHICH YOU THINK EACH WOULD APPLY.

	MILDLY	MODERATELY	MA…
INTROVERTED	⋯	⋯	
EXTROVERTED	⋯	⋯	
SHY	⋯	⋯	
WITHDRAWN	⋯	⋯	
MOODY	⋯	⋯	
DEPRESSIVE	⋯	⋯	
GIVEN TO MOOD SWINGS	⋯	⋯	
ECCENTRIC	⋯	⋯	
GAY	⋯	⋯	
HAPPY	⋯	⋯	
SERIOUS	⋯	⋯	
RESPONSIBLE	⋯	⋯	
CONSCIENTIOUS	⋯	⋯	
IRRESPONSIBLE	⋯	⋯	
EASY-GOING	⋯	⋯	
OTHER DESCRIPTION	⋯	⋯	

SPECIFY ________________________

SOCIAL ATTITUDES AND SELF ASSESSMENT

FRIENDS:		NONE	FEW	M…
	OF SAME SEX	⋯	⋯	
	OF OPPOSITE SEX	⋯	⋯	

THE PATIENT MIXES SOCIALLY

WITH DIFFICULTY ⋯   ADEQUATELY ⋯   EASILY ⋯

THE PATIENT MAKES NEW FRIENDS

WITH DIFFICULTY ⋯   ADEQUATELY ⋯   EASILY ⋯

PATIENT'S SELF DESCRIPTION

IS A HOME LOVING PERSON ⋯   HAS MAINLY FAMILY INTERESTS ⋯

LIKES A VARIED SOCIAL LIFE ⋯   HAS A WELL ORGANIZED SOCIAL LIFE ⋯

HAS A WELL DEVELOPED HOBBY/INTEREST ⋯   HAS TOO MANY INTERESTS ⋯

FEELS SOCIALLY DEPRIVED ⋯   DISAGREES WITH SPOUSE ABOUT SOCIAL ACTIVITIES ⋯

DISAGREES WITH FAMILY ABOUT SOCIAL ACTIVITIES ⋯

FIGURE 7D. DEVELOPMENTAL HISTORY.

this type, such as objective test data, clinician's ratings of patient behavior, or any other type of information leading itself to objectification. Additionally, provisions for the recording of a nineteen character name, the examinee's sex, the month and year of the examinee's birth, up to a nine-digit identification number, from one to sixteen years of education, and a six-digit section for the purpose of assigning any special codes to the data. In the special code section, the clinician could report occupation, marital status, religious affiliation, number of previous patient admissions, or similar data.

Another very useful optical scan form of a multi-purpose nature is the Research Laboratory Data Sheet which is illustrated in Figure 9. On this form, the clinician or researcher could report *summary* psychometric and related data. Four sections are available for the recording of objective test scores (or sociobehavioral indices) with each section having a designation for a three-digit test identification code number and up to four, five-digit scores. The form also has provisions for a two character name designation, the examinee's sex, the date the information was obtained, a provision for a seven-digit hospital identification number, the examinee's age, his weight (in kilograms or pounds), and areas for up to three, four-digit (APA) diagnostic codes. Another section containing four subfields of two digits each can be used for other special data. Finally, the form has an area to indicate the examinee's position in the family. This form can be used as a single input document or one of a series of several documents on a given examinee (a page sequence code is marked on the form).

Both multipurpose optical scan forms (Figures 8 and 9) can serve most any clinical and counseling situation. In the event that the clinician or researcher has input data which a) would not lend itself to objectification on one of these forms, or b) the specific needs of a given computer operation or system require specialized forms, then special forms would have to be designed. As a matter of fact, most computer operations at a given facility or organization use forms designed for their tailor-made needs. On the other hand, if a researcher desires to use the services of a data processing firm which offers time-sharing or one-time contract work, then the most economical way is to adapt one's

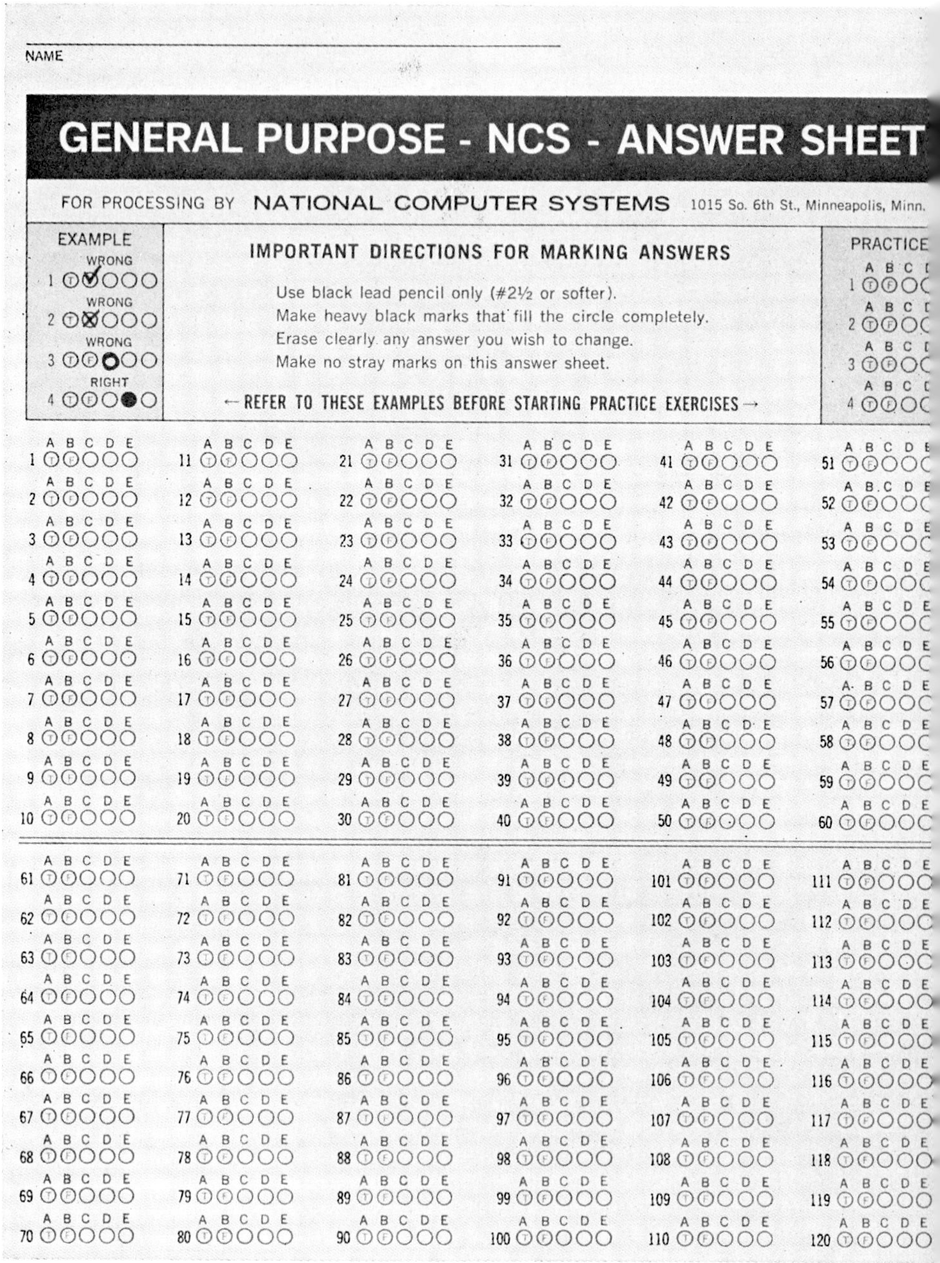

NAME

GENERAL PURPOSE - NCS - ANSWER SHEET

FOR PROCESSING BY **NATIONAL COMPUTER SYSTEMS** 1015 So. 6th St., Minneapolis, Minn.

EXAMPLE

WRONG

PRACTICE

IMPORTANT DIRECTIONS FOR MARKING ANSWERS

Use black lead pencil only (#2½ or softer).
Make heavy black marks that fill the circle completely.
Erase clearly any answer you wish to change.
Make no stray marks on this answer sheet.

← REFER TO THESE EXAMPLES BEFORE STARTING PRACTICE EXERCISES →

FIGURE 8A. GENERAL PURPOSE NCS ANSWER SHEET.

Courtesy of National Computer Systems, 1015 South 6th St., Minneapolis, Minnesota.

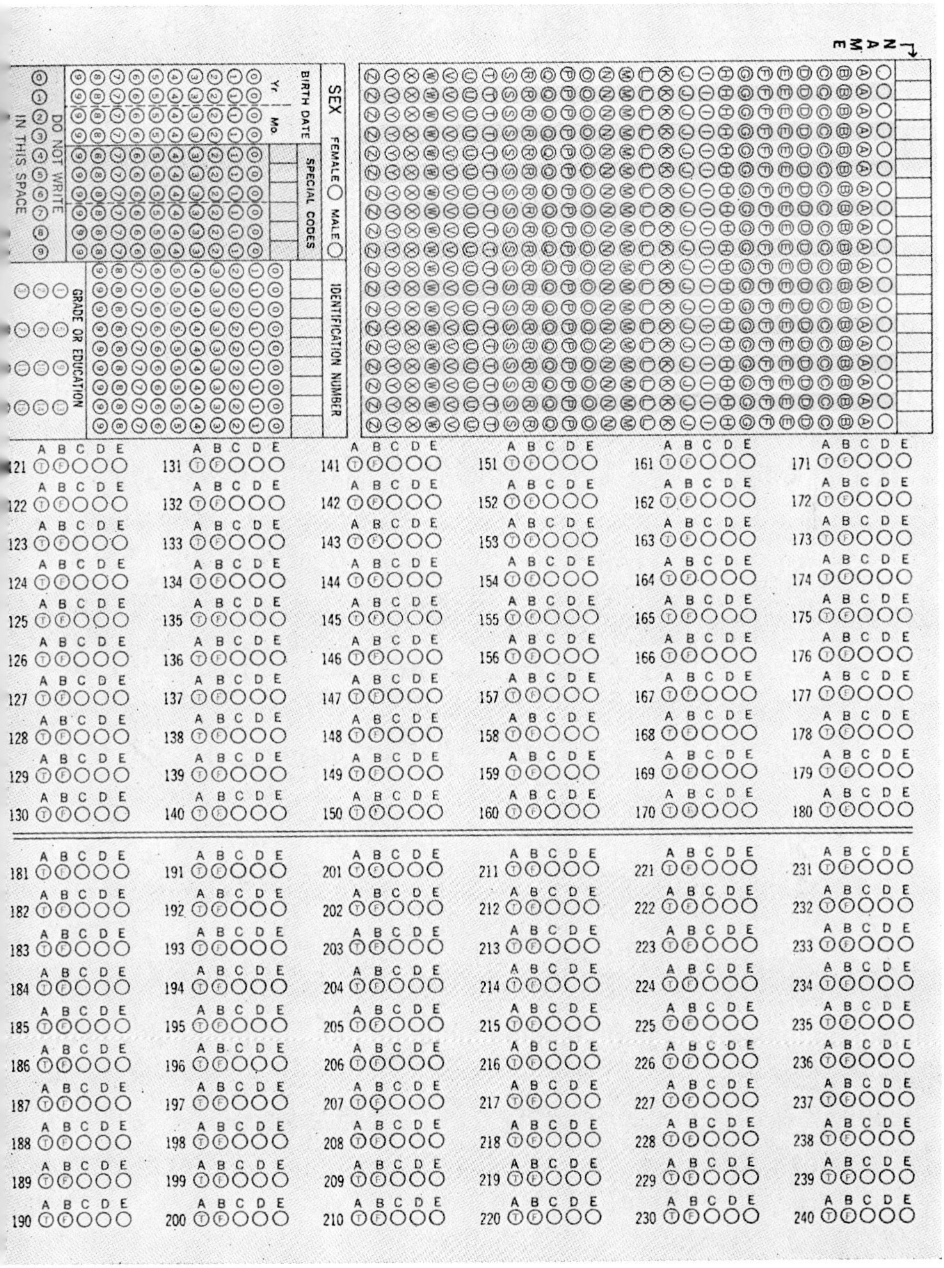

FIGURE 8B. GENERAL PURPOSE NCS ANSWER SHEET.

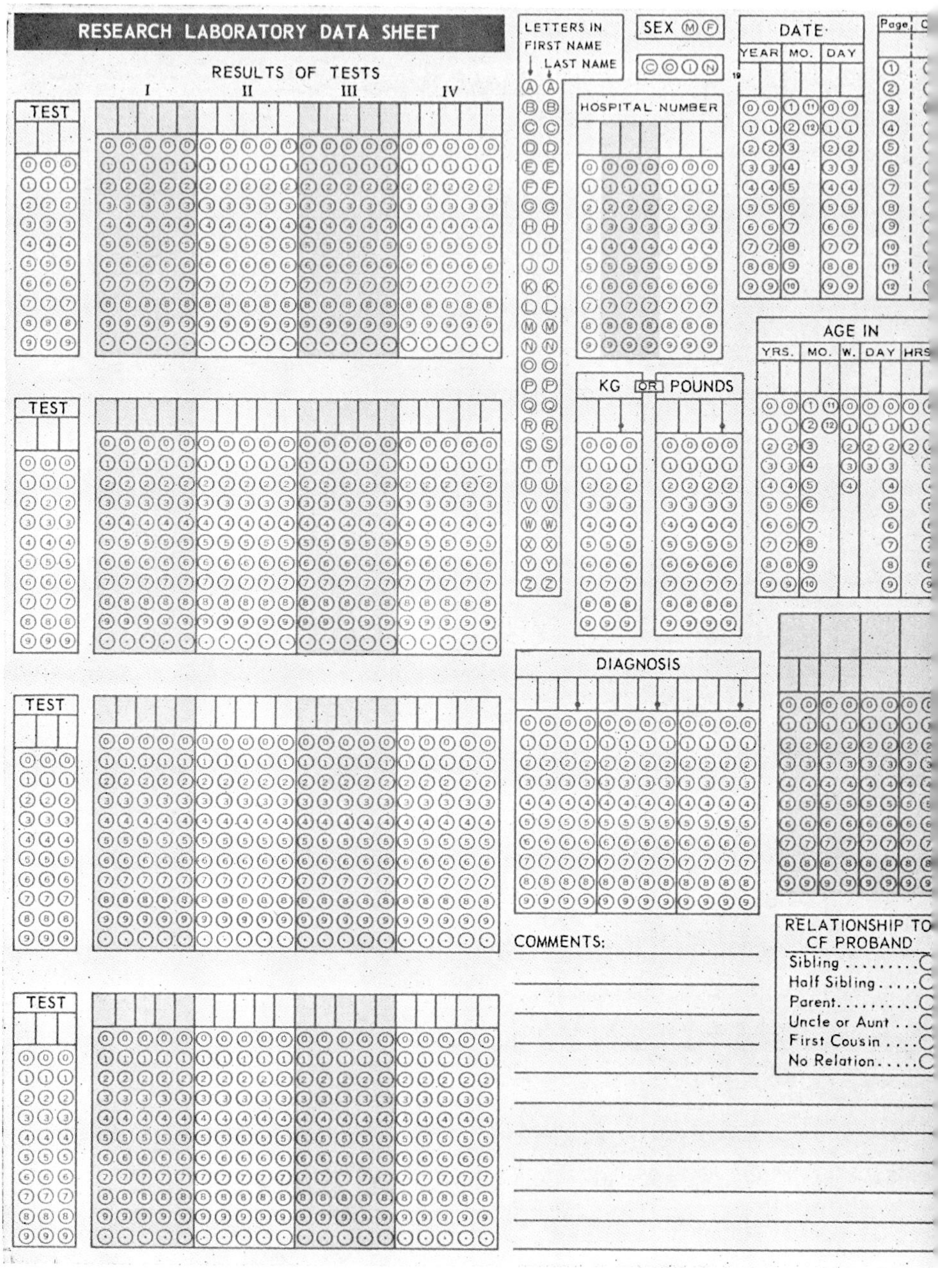

FIGURE 9. RESEARCH LABORATORY DATA SHEET.

Courtesy of National Computer Systems, 1015 South 6th St., Minneapolis, Minnesota.

data to existing forms. These and similar decisions will have to be worked out as specific data processing needs arise, as in reality, there are no forms which are panaceas.

The sample forms presented here are computer-based input media to implement certain specific and general reporting applications. Many other types of forms and data arrangements are limited only by the ability, imagination, and creativity of the clinician, researcher, systems analyst, computer programmer, and the inherent capabilities and limitations of the computer hardware.

This chapter on computerized reporting has not been intended to thoroughly educate the reader in all of the details and parameters of digital computer processes and applications. On the other hand, the reader should have a better general idea of some of the developments in computer technology and related applications in the mental health care field. Additionally, some further knowledge about the input-output formats and requirements of behavioral science reports should have been gained. It is suggested that the reader consult any of the many publications available on computer technology to broaden his familiarity in this area. The professional journals, including those relating to behavioral, physical, medical, and computer science are continuously presenting innovative developments in computer science from which the layman and professional alike can become more familiar.

Suffice to say that even though computer technology has progressed to extremely complex and far-reaching mechanization which is embodied in electronic microcircuitry, it has not become economical enough for each treatment facility and private office to possess one, since costs are thought of in terms of thousands and tens of thousands of dollars for a computer installation. In fact, a small but complete computer center could cost 250,000 dollars to install, staff, and maintain for a period of time. Equipment leasing expense alone can run from 5,000 dollars a month upward. Systems design work, technicians, and software (programs, and the like) supplies can further escalate the cost. A very conservative estimate would be a monthly operating cost of 20,000 dollars to 25,000 dollars for a small computer center, including several major pieces of equipment and a staff of eight to ten persons. Generally, only large treatment facilities and flourishing small private clinics can support a computer center in their organization.

An alternative to this expense is through the popular use of *time-shared* computer services. In time-sharing, a small clinic, agency, research group, or individual can "lease" computer time from other organizations. This time is based upon the actual calculation and processing time required by the computer (computers have built-in timers). A small job might require ten seconds of computer time while a large job could take as long as an hour or so. Also, the purchaser of computer time would pay extra for programming services, card punching, and the like. It would be fairly safe to say that one could purchase a small job run on a company's existing program for as little as 50 dollars. However, most jobs would be more expensive. Going further, some computer service companies and agencies cater entirely to job-oriented activities and therefore charge the user on a job or project basis (many agencies have standard "canned" programs for the more common statistical operations—this saves the researcher a fee for programming). These agencies will also offer consultation services and many have general purpose input forms which the prospective user can purchase. Furthermore, the prospective computer service user might consider the leasing of computer time from a local corporation, for example, one clinic might contract with a large business concern to process their medical records, psychological reports, or statistical data.

Before a given clinician, researcher, or mental health staff in a public or private psychiatric facility or school counseling center begins planning for computer services, it would be worth his time to become familiar with the computerized reports already produced by test scoring companies, test distributors, and special service companies. Achievement and aptitude test batteries which are administered on a large-scale basis are already quite extensively analyzed by the companies selling them. However, most of these large testing companies only report results in terms of percentiles, standard scores, stanines, percentile ranks, means, and the like. But, further statistical calculations on these widely used test instruments are usually available from the testing company or distributor for a few cents extra per report. One test which has been commercially programmed to produce a clinical report in narrative form is the *Minnesota Multiphasic Personality Inventory.* Other such programs may very well be in the developmental stage by the test distributors.

As a matter of fact, some test distributors will assist the test user with custom-designed research programs, and related projects. These services are on a contract basis for various fee schedules. Other companies will assist the prospective user of computer services and reports in the design of input forms and output media. Still other companies such as the computer manufacturers, systems development companies, and management consulting firms will work with one in the design of complete computer systems. Again, there is a service or a specialized company available for virtually every type of computer service for which the user has a specific or comprehensive need.

A prospective user of computer services would do well to ask himself the following questions before he considers "going computer." Do I have sufficient *volume* to justify computerization? Do my needs require *complex*, parametric or nonparametric *statistical calculations* in volume? Do I need *rapid* data analyses for research or other purposes? Do I have the *financial resources* to use computer services? Does the means justify the end? Must my data be *categorized* in complex and multivariant ways? Are my data needs of an *accumulative* or long-range nature? Does my data situation require *extensive* and *routine* calculations and manipulations of data? If the answer is "yes" to any one or more of these questions, computerized assistance *may* be feasible for you or your organization. A computer is not an omnipotent or magical panacea. One only gets what one puts into and instructs the computer to do. You cannot feed a medical textbook, *en toto*, into a computer and expect answers to the mystery of life to suddenly pop out. But, if you tell the computer *how* to treat the data, then you should get an answer the way you want it, if it is a solvable problem.

A list of publications in the area of computer technology is presented in the Appendix. These are specialized publications which the reader should find of interest. Also, a list of computer science journals as well as a list of several computer manufacturers and computer service/consulting firms is given. The reader is encouraged to obtain information in any of these areas and then decide for himself if these publications or services would be of any value to him. However, the author cannot recommend one firm over another.

Chapter XIV

LEGAL IMPLICATIONS OF COMMUNICATION, TESTIMONY, AND REPORTING

CONFIDENTIALITY

A NY FORM of communication, verbal, written, or mechanically recorded can be the object of good will or abuse. The confidentiality of any communication will ultimately depend upon its orignator, intended recipient, and any subsequent disposition. Medical, psychiatric, religious, and legal communications are especially vulnerable to these confidentialities. Aside from any legal ramifications of confidential communications, there are intrinsic moral and ethical bases of which one must take cognizance. The American Personnel and Guidance Association's *Ethical Standards* (Sect. A, para 9) states the following:

> The member has an obligation to ensure that evaluative information about such persons as clients, students, and applicants shall be shared only with those persons who will use such information for professional purposes.

Here, a safeguarding of information on one's client is meant to be intrinsic to the clinician's role.

It has been recognized for some time that the confessions of the parishioner to the priest are held as confidential, if not sacred. The priest is bound by strong moral guidelines not to reveal any information devulged in the Church confessional. The physician is also bound by moral and legal codes not to reveal to others his patient's confidences or the content of his medical or psychiatric record without the expressed permission of the patient. Likewise, the psychiatrist, psychologist, or social worker is governed by moral and ethical restraints not to disclose psychiatric confidences. The lawyer also has certain obligations of confidentiality which he must maintain in order to prevent jeopardy of his client's case.

A portion of the Hippocratic Oath summarizes this concept of confidentiality with a great deal of felicity:

> . . . whatever in connection with my professional practice or not in connection with it, I see or hear in the life of man, which ought not to be spoken of abroad, I will not divulge, thinking that all such should be kept secret.

In keeping with the innovations and farsightedness of the ancient Greeks, Hippocrates very astutely put across this idea around the third century, BC. His ideas became immortal.

PRIVILEGED COMMUNICATION

Within the realm of confidentiality comes the concept of *privileged communication*. By "privileged" one means any client's communication which the recipient is legally allowed to keep silent about when called in a legal proceeding. There is one problem, however. Only certain information is considered to be of a privileged nature, and then only so when held by persons representing certain professional statuses.

Traditionally, only the clergyman and the lawyer have been allowed to remain silent in the courts in regard to client confidences. The lawyer is especially bound to the client's privilege in respect to criminal matters lest he violate his client's right of not testifying against himself as provided for in the Fifth Amendment of the United States Constitution. Additionally, certain information held by a licensed physician or psychiatrist has to some extent been accepted by the courts as privileged.

State laws tend to vary as to *who* may come under the privileged clause. In this respect, Slovenko (1966), pointed out the following:

> A communication is privileged from disclosure in a legal proceeding only when provided by state law. Medical privileged communication is a right existing only by statute. If there is such a statute, a patient may prevent his physician from testifying about his medical treatment and the disclosures which are an integral part of it (p. 6).

It does indicate that universal privilege is not as yet a commonplace occurrence in the Courts. The legal obscurity surrounding the privilege is even more vague if the holder of the information is a psychologist, counselor, or social worker. A myriad of court decisions, pro and con, are not as conclusive as one would like for them to be.

The privilege of the lawyer-client relationship is the most defined and solidified of all. Here, the protection of the Fifth Amendment is sovereign. There is one situation, according to many authorities, where a person other than an attorney can be protected under the lawyer's privilege, so to speak. If the psychiatric professional is examining a client *for* the lawyer, then he is protected by that lawyer's privilege. Thus, the psychiatric examiner is considered to be the lawyer's *agent* or collaborative confidant. This situation came about as the result of a ruling in *City and County of San Francisco vs. Superior Court*, (1951).

THE PSYCHOLOGIST IN COURT

From time to time a psychiatrist, psychologist, or social worker may be asked to testify in court. He may be acting as an agent for the defense or prosecuting attorney, as an "expert" witness, or appointed by the Court to conduct a psychological or psychiatric examination. Since different states and courts will have their own regulations pertaining to psychiatric testimony and evidence, the clinician will do well to familiarize himself with local and state statutes and the limits of privilege. However, it is only fair to mention that there has been and still is a longstanding controversy over the expertise of a "qualified" psychologist. Most of the *opponents*, as expected, seem to come from the physicians, psychiatrists, and prosecuting attorneys (not to mention a few judges) while the *proponents* are the psychologists, defense attorneys, and their allies. Both groups seem to present strong arguments in their own right. And, the courts tend to accept the expertise of the *psychiatrist* more often than that of the psychologist (perhaps for traditional reasons if nothing else); however, this depends upon the opinion of the judge in a particular situation. This inequity seems to stem, for the most part, from archaic traditions set by the medical profession and their supporters. This will be explained more in a later discussion.

The clinician may be summoned to testify in divorce, child custody, personal injury, probate, insurance, military, sanity, criminal, or restoration of civil rights cases (Slovenko, 1966). In each of these situations the quantity and specificity of the clinician's testimony will be contingent upon the nature of the case being heard or tried.

Before the realm of court proceedings are discussed further, an important point should be emphasized. A distinction is made between *psychotherapeutic sessions* (one-to-one and group models) which are considered to contain privileged information, and *psychiatric evaluative procedures* which are *not* considered to be privileged.

Irrespective of any court's ruling or State statutes, the psychotherapy session usually involves a disclosure of interpersonal and intrapsychiac interactions which are considered by the clinician to be confidential communication. On the other hand, *interpretations* of interview and psychometric data contain basically the examiner's *opinion*, and professional *opinions* are not privileged per se. Next, if a client or patient initiates court proceedings and asks a clinician to testify in his behalf, then the privilege may be waived. Perhaps a client who initiates a psychiatric hearing feels he has nothing to hide, or that it may be to his advantage to make public his conversations with the psychologist or psychiatrist.

Psychologists and Psychiatrists

Who, then, is qualified to testify as an expert witness, conduct a psychiatric examination at the request of the court, or to evaluate a client's mental status? The laws are somewhat varied and at times obscure on this point.

Apparently, one problem seems to come from the European psychoanalytic precedent established by Sigmund Freud and other psychoanalysts who were also physicians. This medical model still lingers in our courts in many states. That is, in some states unless you are a physician you cannot be asked to serve as an "expert" witness, regardless of your professional qualifications. Fortunately, as of June, 1968, some thirty-seven states provided for statutory certification or licensing of *psychologists* and *psychological examiners* with thirty-two of these states granting the psychiatric privilege to clients of psychologists thereby licensed or certified (Hildreth, 1968). As yet, social workers and marriage counselors (unless they are first a qualified psychologist) are not protected by the privilege. The states which provide for registration, certification, or licensing are as follows:

*	Alabama	(P)			Minnesota	
*	Alaska	(P)			Mississippi	(P)
	Arizona	(P)		*	Nebraska	(P)
*	Arkansas	(P)			Nevada	(P)
	California	(P)			New Hampshire	(P)
*	Colorado	(P)		*	New Jersey	(P)
	Connecticut				New Mexico	(P)
	Delaware	(P)			New York	(P)
	Florida	(P)		*	North Carolina	(P)
*	Georgia	(P)			North Dakota	
	Hawaii			*	Oklahoma	(P)
*	Idaho	(P)			Oregon	(P)
	Illinois	(P)		*	South Carolina	
	Kansas	(P)		*	Tennessee	(P)
*	Kentucky	(P)			Utah	(P)
	Louisiana	(P)		*	Virginia	(P)
*	Maine	(P)			Washington	(P)
	Maryland	(P)			Wyoming	(P)

Note: * —Special Licensing Act; not the same as registration or certification.
   P —Acknowledges the Privilege.

As a rule, only a licensed, certified, or registered psychologist can function as an *expert* witness, subject to state statutes and local Court rulings. In some cases, a "nonexpert" (not licensed, etc.) can conduct a psychiatric evaluation requested by the Court; however, any such evaluation would usually be supervised by a qualified (licensed, etc.) psychological examiner, psychologists, or psychiatrist.

Two classic insanity cases, *M'Naghten* in England, and *Durham* in the United States, have been the bases for many court decisions in American law. The first emphasized a "right or wrong" aspect of criminal intent; the latter, the "mental disease or defect" concept. Both cases involved strong medical models of mental disease and these rulings have produced an unnecessary lag in establishing the role of the psychologist as an expert witness in the courts. There have been dozens of cases in the courts over these precedents. They can be reduced to the fact that the courts generally consider mental illness to be a *disease* and that no person can *diagnose* or *treat* a "disease" except a physician, psychiatrist, alienist, or any combination thereof.

A specific case in forensic psychology was illustrated in *People vs. Hawthorne*, (1940). A highly qualified Ph.D. clinical psychologist, who was an educator and learned clinician, was not allowed to "diagnose" a case of *sanity* because he was *not a physician* with medical training and therefore could not diagnose a *disease*! This was not the first and will most assuredly not be the last controversy of this type in American jurisprudence. In response to *Jenkins vs. United States*, (1959) the American Psychological Association filed an *amicus curiae* brief on January 19, 1962 (the American Psychiatric Association filed one also) in the United States Court of Appeals in the District of Columbia challenging the issue of "who is qualified." In reporting this brief, Hoch and Darley (1962, p. 626) noted that the qualifications and expertise of "properly qualified psychologists in cases involving the determination and meaning of mental disease or defect as productive of criminal acts" were sufficient in most instances to diagnose and treat mental disorders in lieu of *medical* training per se. The Court of Appeals upheld the *amicus curiae* brief by a vote of seven to two. In *State vs. Tull*, (1965) a psychologist was not allowed to testify in a murder case. So, as the reader will see the law is rather complex and at times inconsistent when it comes to forensic psychology.

What is Privileged?

As mentioned previously, state laws usually decide *who* is protected by the client's privilege and *what* information is of a privileged nature. Depending upon these conditions, both verbal and written testimony (or other recorded media) may come under the privileged clause. It should be remembered that what constitutes confidentiality or privilege in the eyes of the psychologist or psychiatrist may *not* be deemed so in the courts. It is unfortunate that this discrepancy exists between the moral-ethical and the legal codes.

A general distinction can be made in that confidences between the clinician and his client are considered of a privileged nature where provided for by State law. The same is true of medical and psychiatric records. On the other hand, psychiatric *examinations* relating to mental status and competency when requested by police authorities or the court, are not considered to be privileged; they are not a private voluntary communiqué from a client to his therapist (Slovenko, 1966).

In *Taylor vs. United States*, (1951) it was held that *prima facie* evidence obtained by a prosecuting attorney's psychiatrist was a violation of both the Fifth Amendment and the privilege. Therefore, the psychologist or psychiatrist is *not* required (and should not be asked) to disclose any *admissions* made by the defendant during the course of examination lest the defendant's constitutional rights be violated. The clinician *may*, however, give his professional *opinion* or evaluation of the defendant without jeopardizing his rights. This will hold true in both criminal and civil cases.

The rights of the defendant are held to be above any other needs of the Court. In criminal cases the defendant is especially guarded against self-incrimination. The same holds true for civil cases. But, there is always a possibility of unnecessary slander, even on the witness stand. For the most part, the decision as to *what* is considered privileged is left up to the courts, keeping in mind the inherent rights of the defendant. Louisell (1957) noted that any patient or client who has a right to obtain psychiatric help in any form also has an equivalent right to have his communications privileged. Grold (1968), in discussing problems of confidentiality, stressed that the traditional concepts of confidentiality were outmoded in terms of the newer socio-therapeutic interactions and milieu therapy in general.

Psychological Records

The psychological report also comes under the auspices of the State laws, and the laws differ among the states. If no privilege exists in a given state, then the entire medical record (including all psychological material) is subject to court subpoena (Slovenko, 1966).

Whenever records on a given client are being considered for use in court, the person in charge of the records should use discretion so that undue harm will not come to the defendant. Of course, if the holder of these records has been subpoened by the court to supply such records, and if he fails to do so, then he could be held in contempt of court. Assuming that the holder of the records has a choice as to what to present in court, an ethical guideline might be the following statement in the American Personnel and Guidance Association's *Ethical Standards* (Sect. B, para. 3, 1961).

> Records of the counseling relationship including interview notes, test data, correspondence, tape recordings, and other documents are considered professional information for use in counseling, research, and teaching of counselors but always with full protection of the identity of the client and with precaution so that no harm will come to him.

Quite naturally, a client or defendant's name will be revealed on any case appearing in the Courts. On the other hand, one should use his professional judgment as to whether or not certain information would infringe upon the inherent rights of the defendant. Again, the distinction should be made between therapeutic and evaluative data. Noyes and Kolb (1963) stressed that the physician in Court should not use any information about his client without his client's expressed permission, unless prohibited by statute.

There is a long-standing precedent in the Courts as to the nature of *factual* and *hearsay* evidence. For the most part, factual evidence is direct observation and hearsay is what a third party said. This situation can very well present problems in the courts. Verbatim recordings of a client's statements during a psychotherapy session may be admitted as factual evidence in the courts; however, the state of confidentiality may be violated. Results of psychological tests may also be admitted as evidence. And, the witnessing of concrete events can be admitted as a certain type of evidence. Theoretical analyses and interpretations of case history, interview, and psychometric data are not considered to be evidence. They are merely testimony and may in some instances be considered hearsay testimony at best.

On the Witness Stand

The "expert" witness such as a psychologist or psychiatrist is allowed to give his *opinion* about a case unlike the lay witness. The expert's function is to present the data, and give an opinion based only on that data. The psychological evidence and the ensuing interpretation should be of a first-hand nature; otherwise it may be discounted by the court as opinion evidence.

Furthermore, a qualified expert, having never seen the defendant prior to the trial or hearing (as well as a nonexpert who *may* have worked with or evaluated the client)* may be called on the stand to give a professional opinion based on a "hypothetical" situation (Guttmacher and Weihofen, 1952). As a result, the attorneys may pose a hypothetical question such as, "in a given situation, if facts A + B + C were present, what would be the probable outcome or conclusion?" A technique such as this could very well be used to color the trial and to sway the jurors feelings toward favor or disfavor of the client and defendant.

With respect to the confidentiality of the psychotherapeutic relationship, Slovenko (1966, p. 47) pointed out the following:

> The patient in psychotherapy has the task of revealing his private personality, the personality which exists behind the social facade. Incongruous attitudes emerge which are completely at variance with the patient's everyday-functioning personality. Their production is necessary in treatment but devastating if revealed to public scrutiny.

The essence here seems to be that a client's "private" or intra-psychic personality is somewhat different from his "everyday-functioning personality." How true. Thus, the *inner life* of a client may be related to his action-oriented observable behavior but an *a priori* relationship between these two realms cannot be empirically demonstrated to any substantial degree. In other words, for one to *fantasize* about murdering someone does not necessarily mean that the physical act will occur. Going further, Slovenko (1966, p. 47) commented:

---

* Material in parenthesis that of this author.

Data from free-association, fantasies, or memories are not reliable for use in court as they primarily represent the way the person experienced an event, and not how the event occurred. They are not "facts."

As a result, fantasies, free-associations, memories, and other intrapsychic interactions per se are *not facts* and do not meet any form of empirically demonstrated cause-effect criteria. Subsequently, these abstractions constitute a type of hearsay evidence in the Courts. On the other side of the coin, if a client says, for example, "If I had the chance I would kill Mr. X," then this *admission of intent* on the part of the client would constitute a *factual verbal statement* and, becomes a *factual event* only if the act is carried out. One will undoubtedly recall that a client or defendant's *admissions* of actual or intended criminal acts during a psychotherapeutic interaction cannot be used as evidence against the client under violation of the self-incrimination clause. In situations such as these the client would be protected by either the privilege, the Fifth Amendment of the Constitution, or both. In actual practice the nature about a specific situation may not be as explicit.

Mental Competency

In past years, many patients who were committed to a public mental institution lost their civil rights. The person bringing charges of mental, behavioral, or physical incompetence against a member of his family or citizen of the community did so for several possible reasons. Some individuals were confined for aberrant and acting-out social behavior, some for a severe lack of socialization, some for intellectual defects, and still others for physical handicaps. In any number of instances the victim of involuntary commitment should not have been confined by our present-day standards. Nevertheless, many of these patients lost their civil rights as the result of a Court ruling. This left the patient helpless to help himself and subsequently at the mercy of society which did not always have the patient's welfare and best interests foremost in view. In some instances (perhaps more so than some wish to admit) a family member was committed to an institution for the "insane," his civil rights taken away, and then the relatives began their unscrupulous task of claiming the patient's estate under the guise of "doing what's best."

In recent years an attempt has been made by various persons and psychiatric facilities to regain many patients' civil rights so that they may be better prepared to function as a citizen in the community. In order to restore a patient's civil rights, he must be restored to mental competency. This usually requires a psychiatric examination by one or more persons and a court hearing. Since many patients in the public mental institutions are indigent, they must possess their civil rights in order to qualify for Public Aid or Public Assistance payments after they have been discharged from the hospital. In some cases, where the patient has no family members living, a *conservator* must be appointed to aid the patient in regaining his civil rights. Unfortunately, few persons are willing to assist with the procedures without monetary compensation for their efforts. If the patient is indigent the problem is further accentuated since the conservator will be required to pay certain expenditures for the legal processes.

To further infringe upon the institutionalized patient, his psychotherapeutic interactions and his medical records are not considered privileged in some states. This is especially true if the patient has lost his civil rights as he is considered a ward of the State. Robitscher (1966) commented that the hospitalized mental patient did not have the right "in many jurisdictions" to *demand* a psychiatric examination upon admission, much less to have any records kept confidential. Fortunately, most hospitals maintain the rights of privilege of their patients' communications and records and consider these to be intrinsically confidential. A number of states have passed laws that require prompt psychiatric examinations for all newly admitted patients; furthermore, in any number of jurisdictions the legal statutes specify periodic follow-up evaluations for each patient at specified intervals. Irrespective of *who* the patient is, or *where* he is receiving treatment his confidences and records should be maintained as privileged communication.

The psychologist or psychiatrist will on occasion be called to testify as to a client's mental competency or sanity. This is especially true in criminal trials. In the third century AD, a Roman jurist, Domitius Ulpianus, stated that an insane person cannot be held responsible for any crimes which he may commit. Later, an Englishman, Henry de Bracton (ca. 13th century), concurred with Ulpianus' belief on the issue of criminal responsibility (Alexander and Selesnick, 1966, p. 349).

In 1843 Daniel M'Naghten was acquitted on a murder charge after being declared "insane." He had shot and killed a man in the "mistaken belief" that the man was someone else. The reader will recall that this case was the basis for the "right and wrong" test of criminal responsiblity. Later, the decision of the Durham case (1954) ruled that the right-wrong test of insanity was not adequate and that the *psychiatrist* should establish whether or not the criminal act was due to mental *disease* or *defect* (Noyes and Kolb, 1963; Slovenko, 1966). The M'Naghten rule only considered the cognitive aspect of the mind and did not subscribe to the significance of any emotional or behavioral phenomena (Alexander and Slesnick, 1966, p. 349).

The American Law Institute's *Model Penal Code* discounts the Durham ruling, in part, on the grounds that an "act" is not necessarily the "product" of mental disease or defect (Robitscher, 1966, p. 61). Obviously, these and other legal statements tend to be quite divergent. But, these remain significant issues in the Courts as well as in the forensic literature.

In certain cases the psychologist or psychiatrist may be asked to examine a client to determine if he is competent to stand trial. This seems to be somewhat of an ambiguous process inasmuch as it appears more so to be a question of the client's sanity or insanity. A somewhat more definitive and significant question is whether or not the defendant was insane *at the time of* the criminal act, which goes back to the rationale used in the M'Naghten and Durham cases. Obviously, any *post facto* psychiatric examination cannot ascertain the true status of the defendant's *ante facto* cognition with any substantial degree of certainty. One can only gather the existing "facts," subjectively interpret them, and speculate as to the mental state of a person before and during the commission of a crime. Since emotional and motivational processes are seldom *ad hoc* phenomena (even though it is possible) one must assume that behavior and cognitive processes are continuing and relatively predictable mechanisms which are probably in operation prior to, during, and following an antisocial act.

Despite many legal procedures used by lawyers, physicians, and the Courts to seek commitment or discharge of a mental patient, the examining psychiatrist usually has the final say as to the patient's need for treatment. Psychologists are rapidly gaining status in the eyes of the Courts for this traditional, but perhaps antiquated, function of the psychiatrist. Nevertheless, the final decision by psychiatric personnel is usually upheld by the Courts. However, the Court may request that if and when the patient is found to be sane that he be discharged to the guardianship of the Court or its agent so that the ex-patient can serve any previously imposed sentence for a crime.

Pre-sentencing Reports

In criminal cases, pre-sentencing psychological and psychiatric reports may be requested by the Court. Here, the Court may wish to know a) if the defendant is mentally competent, or b) if incarceration in a penal institution would be more or less desirable than confinement in a mental institution. The same question may come up in a pre-trial sanity hearing. The issue of pre-sentencing reports has been brought up in the cases of *Morgan vs. State* (1962), *Smith vs. United States* (1959), *United States vs. Chrisos* (1961), and *Williams vs. New York* (1948). Each of these decisions seems to indicate that the pre-sentencing report infringes upon the constitutional rights of the defendant.

When there is a *death penalty* imposed upon the defendant for a capital crime, the convicted person *must be found sane* before the execution can be carried out. Generally, if a person is insane he will be found so prior to sentencing. In some cases the person may "go insane" *after* sentencing, as some may allege. Here, the issue of post-sentencing insanity can be raised by the person having custody of the prisoner. In a decision reached in *Sloesbee vs. Balkcom* (1950), it was concluded that the prisoner's exemption from the death penalty by reason of *post facto* insanity is a "grace" and not a "right." Furthermore, the State is not *obliged* to allow this type of a sanity hearing without a just cause (Slovenko, 1966).

RELEASES OF CONFIDENTIAL INFORMATION

Any psychological or medical data on a client or patient being held by private practitioners, a public or private mental hospital, or an out-patient clinic should be considered highly confidential. Only those professional members of a given diagnostic or treatment facility should have routine access to this information. Even then, the information should *only* be used for the welfare of the client and *not* for the personal enlightenment of the staff members.

Despite any legal issues over who can diagnose, treat, or function as an expert witness, the inherent nature of psychiatric and medical records is another matter. And, any indiscriminate release of this written or mechanically recorded information (audio or video tape-recorded, computer stored, microfilmed, etc.) can open the door to serious if not expensive lawsuits and related repercussions. Few would find this appealing.

Generally, there are certain governmental agencies which may request copies of confidential information. Therefore, the hospitals, clinics, or private practitioners who possess clinical records on their patients or clients are obligated to furnish any requested information to the following agencies, unless specifically prohibited by subsequent legislation which abrogates that previously enacted.

1. Federal Bureau of Investigation.
2. Railroad Retirement Administration.
3. Social Security Administration.
4. United States Secret Service.
5. Veteran's Administration.

These five Federal agencies may *inspect* any confidential data at any time, as provided for under Federal law. If a state mental health agency or department compiles medical records data, a Federal agency does not have *free license* to peruse one or more confidential records at will, *unless* the Federal agency can show *just cause* for examining one or more individual patient records.

Additionally, the State Department of Public Aid and the Federal Department of Health, Education, and Welfare can examine records to ascertain benefits allocable to patients under Medicare and Title XIX programs.

One is *not obligated* to furnish information to the following agencies or individuals:

1. Private individuals (including family members).
2. Professional persons (not employed by the record-holding facility).
3. Private agencies.
4. Business concerns.
5. Employers (past, present, and future).

A consent for release of confidential information should be obtained from the patient, guardian, parent, conservator, or legal representative of the patient, prior to the releasing of any confidential records to these persons or agencies which do not come under State or Federal control.

Certain limited information may be supplied to other agencies or persons without an official consent for release of confidential information from the patient or his legal representative. This information is generally limited to answers to such question as, "Is or is not the party a patient or client?" and similar questions. Private agencies or individuals, including friends, relatives, employers, the police, and others are included in this category. The holder of the clinical records will have to use his own judgment as to what information should be released without an official release form having been obtained. The individual or agency holding the records should not release any information to "questionable" persons or agencies, especially if a signed release has not been obtained from the patient or his legal advisor or representative. It is always a good practice to obtain consent from the patient or his representative in any event. Requests from the military, other hospitals and clinics, and similar agencies should be filled subject to obtaining a signed release.

A patient may wish that general or specific details of his treatment or hospitalization be withheld from his family, friends, family doctor, minister, employer, and others. This request from the patient should be honored in all cases unless the withholding of this information would endanger the well-being of the patient or others. This particular point was illustrated by Grold (1968) where the question of whether or not a psychiatrist had the right to violate the privilege with a patient who had informed him of his use of marijuana during his hospital stay. For the psychiatrist to remain silent would tend to have an approving or reinforcing effect upon the patient's behavior as well as allowing the continuance of a violation of the narcotics law.

In research applications one seldom needs to know the identity of a patient, only a case number is usually necessary. There are exceptions, though. In the few instances when a name must be used for inclusion in results which are to be circulated to the reading public, then the patient's consent should be obtained in writing. The careless researcher could easily encourage a lawsuit against himself (or his employer) if he uses names, photographs, or easily identifiable demographic information in reporting his research findings. This is to say nothing of the personal slander or embarrassment the client or patient might suffer.

With the advent of computerization of psychological and medical records data, another concept has been brought into view. This concerns the electronic *storage* and *retrieval* of confidential material, in narrative or coded statistical form. With computer storage, the medical records department at a given facility no longer has the complete control over the records since the data are processed by computer personnel who are not necessarily medical records employees. Therefore, the data processing personnel will necessarily become secondary (or perhaps primary) guardians of confidential records through their safeguarding of data output and storage. The obvious responsibilities of computer personnel were especially emphasized by Fitzgibbon (1966) in terms of psychological test information. Additionally, the forthcoming expansion of computer usage by many facilities will undoubtedly alter many traditionally operated medical records departments. Thus far, most medical records have become just that, records. A mental health agency can greatly expand its uses of data from medical and psychiatric records with a computer installation or time-shared services. This is especially true in research applications.

Consent of Release

The reader will undoubtedly be cognizant of the fact that if a patient or client is intellectually, emotionally, and physically capable of signing a release form (and understanding its content) that he must do so. If a patient is a minor, then his parent or guardian must sign the release. In the event that a patient has been previously declared incompetent by the Court and he has lost his civil rights, then his conservator or other legal representative with the power of attorney should sign the release. However, the patient may be asked to sign the form anyway as a matter of record.

In certain instances where a patient has been classified by the examining psychologist or psychiatrist as being harmful to himself or to others, then the psychiatric facility may release confidential information to law enforcement or other personnel in order to avert a catastrophe. This may be a delicate issue in some jurisdictions as some local rulings or state statutes may not sanction this action. In any event, a psychiatric facility may alert law enforcement personnel of a patient's condition if the patient has left the facility without hospital authorization, if it is felt that he committed an act of violence. Whether or not a private practitioner is morally, ethically, or legally obligated to report a *possible* deviant or criminal action to the authorities is a controversial issue. It becomes an issue of what is more important and ethical, the protection of society or the safeguarding of the patient's rights under the legal privilege and the United States Constitution.

Types of Release Forms

Authorizations for release of confidential information may be of any format or design. The essential elements of any release form are the following: a) the name of the client or patient, b) the name of the holder of the records, c) the name of the requesting agency or individual, d) the nature of the material to be released, e) the date of the release, f) the signature of the patient, or his parent, guardian, conservator, or legal representative, and g) the signatures of the patient or his representative and one or more witnesses.

Figure 10 illustrates one type of "Authorization for Release of Information." This form includes a blanket release for all information during the inclusive dates of the patient's hospitalization.

When a Court requests and receives any medical or psychiatric records, a form such as shown in Figure 11 may be used. Note that a checklist format for the "Receipt of Original Medical Records" is used in this particular form in order to indicate report and/or record specificity. However, this format of a checklist is

---

FIGURE 10. AUTHORIZATION FOR RELEASE OF INFORMATION.

Courtesy of Physician's Record Company. From Huffman, E. K.: *Manual for Medical Record Librarians.* Physician's Record Company, Berwyn, Ill., p. 432, 1963.

To_______________________________ Hospital No._____________
      (Name of Hospital)

You are hereby authorized to furnish such professional information, in accordance with the policy of your hospital, to _________________________
                              (Name of Recipient)

from the medical records compiled during my hospitalization from ___________19_____ to ____________19______, and are hereby released from all legal liability that may arise from the release of the information requested.

Date _____________   (Signed)_____________________________
                              (Patient or nearest of kin)

(Signed)_____________________________
    (Party inspecting record)   (Relationship if signed by other than patient)

Date of inspection of record _____________19_____

(Signed)_____________________________ (or)
    (Attending physician)

(Signed)_____________________________
    (Psychologist)

Note: Authorization must be signed by the patient, or by the nearest relative in the case of a minor or when the patient is physically or mentally incompetent.

not essential. A provision is also included in this form for a Court's clerk to sign it, thereby indicating receipt of the given records. A form such as this could be used by any agency receiving confidential records or parts thereof.

FIGURE 11. RECEIPTS FOR ORIGINAL MEDICAL RECORDS.

Courtesy of Physician's Record Company. Adapted from the original by Huffman, E. K.: *Manual for Medical Record Librarians.* Physician's Record Company, Berwyn, Ill., p. 428, 1963.

Date_____________

Received of ____
　　　　　　　　　　　　(Name of Hospital)

____Medical Record or Case No.
　　　　　　(Address of Hospital)

__________ of_______________________________consisting of a total of _________
　　　　　　　　　(Name of Patient)

sheets.

_______ Summary Sheet	_______ Reports of Anesthesia
_______ Personal Identification Sheet	_______ Reports of Operation
_______ History Sheet	_______ X-Ray Reports
_______ Physical Examination Sheet	_______ Psychological Evaluation
_______ Physician's Order Sheets	_______ Psychiatric Examination
_______ Progress Note Sheets	_______ _______________________
_______ Nurses' Bedside Record Sheets	_______ _______________________
_______ Graphic Sheets	_______ _______________________
_______ Urinalysis Reports	_______ _______________________
_______ Blood Count Reports	_______ _______________________
_______ Bacteriological Reports	_______ _______________________
_______ EEG Reports	_______ _______________________
_______ EKG (or ECG) Reports	_______ _______________________

This record will be returned to ____
　　　　　　　　　　　　　　　　　(Name of Hospital)

_________________________________on_____________ marked for
　　　　　(Address of Hospital)　　　　(Date for Return)

the the attention of _______________________________, Medical Records Librarian.

(Signed)_______________________

Clerk of_______________________Court, Room No._______

Phone No._______________________

Another sample release form, "Consent for Release of Confidential Information," is shown in Figure 12. Again, a blanket release is used. In this form, a provision for a witness to sign it is included, which may be either the person obtaining the release, the person sending the records, or a third party.

Researchers who anticipate the use of confidential material derived from tape recordings, video tape recordings, photographs, or films which is to be distributed for circulation or publication should plan to obtain a release. If in any manner the patient is identifiable then a release is mandatory. A sample form, "Consent for Photographing or Mechanically Recording," is shown in Figure 13.

With the increased impetus of state, national, and international plans for research *Data Banks*, a release form which is directed toward this situation would seem to be appropriate. In fact, sev-

---

FIGURE 12. CONSENT FOR RELEASE OF CONFIDENTIAL INFORMATION.

I,__________________________, hereby give my written consent to have
   (Name of Patient)

the__________________________________at________________________________
  (Name of Hospital or Agency)   (Address)
release all pertinent medical and psychological/psychiatric information
which pertains to my case to the____
           (Name of Receiving Agency)

at__________________________________. I furthermore release all
   (Address)
parties stated herewithin from any legal liability resulting from the release of this information, with the understanding that all parties involved will exercise sufficient safeguards while using this information.

Date of Consent____________19_____

(Signed)_________________________ (or)
    (Patient)

(Signed)_________________________
   (Legal Representative)

Address_______________________

Witness_______________________Address_______________________

Witness_______________________Address_______________________ eral of these Data Banks are in operation at this time. Any number of problems might arise when multitudes of research data, including the patient's identity, are funneled into these organizations. In particular, a decision will have to be reached as to *who may retrieve* data from the computer storage, and *who may receive* the information. For the most part, any retrieved data would probably be in group statistical form, thereby preserving the identity of a given patient. A special form to be used by a researcher who plans to submit confidential information to a computer Data Bank is shown in Figure 14, "Consent for Data Bank Storage." Whether or not a form of this type would be necessary in a given situation will ultimately depend upon State and Federal legislation, the standards maintained by the Data Banks, and the type of identifying information contained in the research data.

FIGURE 13. CONSENT FOR PHOTOGRAPHING OR MECHANICALLY RECORDING.

I,________________________, hereby give my written consent to
    (Name of Patient)

______________________________at the________________________________
   (Name of Clinician)   (Name and Address of Facility)

to use for research, instructional, or publication purposes any
_______________________________ made of me while engaged in ward, hospital,
(Specify the type of media)

or clinic activities, or individual and group psychotherapy sessions during my stay at the above named facility. I further understand that my name or picture may be used in these instructional, research, or publication media and that by signing this release I give my permission for this to be done. Furthermore, I release the photographer,_______________________, and/or the mechanical technician,_______________________, as well as the above-named clinician and facility (clinic, hospital, or other) from any and all liability resulting from the use of these materials for the aforementioned professional purposes.

Date of Consent____________19_____ (Signed)________________________
                                     (Patient)

Witness:________________________Address________________________

Witness:________________________Address________________________

Witness:________________________Address________________________

The information conveyed in this chapter should provide the reader with a general knowledge of the legal aspects of psychological reporting, both in written reports and in the courtroom. Inasmuch as there is a paucity of information available on specific court rulings, and controversies between the psychiatrists' and the psychologists' standings in these realms, the interested reader is encouraged to seek other literature in the area of forensic psychiatry. A few specialized references are listed at the end of this chapter for the reader's convenience.

Some psychologists and psychiatrists will never be asked to serve as an "expert witness" in the Courts. Some will never testify in a psychiatric case. On the other hand, *all* psychologists

---

FIGURE 14. CONSENT FOR DATA BANK STORAGE.

I,________________________________, hereby give my written consent to have
    (Name of Patient)

any diagnostic, psychotherapeutic, medical, psycholometric, socioeconomic, sociobehavioral, or demographic information on file in regard to my case at the________________________,________________________________, be
    (Name of Agency)   (Address)

supplied to the ____________________Data Bank or to the ____________________Research Institute, at________________________________
    (Address of Data Bank or other)

for use in local, state, national, or international research compilations and analyses. Furthermore, I release the ________________________________
    (Name of present record holding agency)

at ____________________________ and the following clinician
    (Address)

(if applicable)____________________ from all legal liability resulting
    (Name of Clinician)

from the release and subsequent dissemination of this information. I, the undersigned patient, understand that the abovementioned Data Bank or Research Institute will have copies of materials from these records and that they will exercise the controls of confidentiality upon these data as deemed necessary by their organization's professional standards.

Date of Consent:____________   (Signed)________________
           (Patient)

Witness:____________   Address________________

and psychiatrists (as well as other professional clinicians) should be aware of certain moral, ethical, and legal problems in the use and subsequent disclosure of privileged communication. As a final note, any psychiatric testimony presented in the Courts becomes common property of the people and a matter of public record.

SUGGESTED READING LIST

1. American Psychological Association: *Ethical Standards for Psychologists*. Washington, D.C., APA, 1953.
2. Geiser, R. L., and Rheingold, P. D.: Psychology and the legal process: Testimonial privileged communications. *Amer Psychol, 19*:831-837, 1964.
3. Hess, J. H., and Thomas, H. E.: Incompetency to stand trial. *Amer J Psychiat, 119*:713-720, 1963.
4. Jeffery, R.: The psychologist as an expert witness on the issue of insanity. *Amer Psychol, 19*:838-843, 1964.
5. Leifer, R.: The psychiatrist and tests of criminal responsibility. *Amer Psychol, 19*:825-830, 1964.
6. Weihoffen, H.: *Insanity as a Defense in Criminal Law*. New York, Commonwealth Fund, 1933.
7. Wiseman, F.: Psychiatry and the law: Use and abuse of psychiatry in a murder case. *Amer J Psychiat, 118*:289-299, 1961.
8. Entire issue of *Psychology Today*, February, 1969.

Chapter XV

OVERVIEW

FEW WRITERS have the ability to prepare a perfect report the first time around. Most of us find it necessary to prepare a rough draft of our information, read it, then begin to make the necessary corrections. Most reports of any merit are *rewritten*, not written.

There are many details one must review in order to produce a scholarly psychological report. Items of grammar such as spelling, sentence structure, phrasing, vocabulary usage and level, use of idioms, and continuity of content are often overlooked by some writers. The good report will sound good as well as read easily. The best reports will *communicate* in a clear and concise manner. Reports which ramble in a haphazard fashion are scarcely more informative than handing the reader your raw, unassembled data.

As pointed out earlier, one must have all of the pertinent facts on one's client present before an intelligent report can be written. Then, these facts should be organized in a systematic and logical fashion. The content of the psychological report should then lead to a diagnosis and recommendations for treatment follow-up, discharge planning, or referral. A report can be an invaluable tool for other clinicians if it does its inherent job—communicate. And, communication is the *sine qua non* of effective writing. Few individuals will enjoy reading a report which is so replete with verbosity that a dictionary must be used to understand its content. Therefore, do not attempt to impress your reader with a grandiose vocabulary and paragraph length sentences. Be creative! Be simple! Communicate!

Another trap which one can inadventently succumb to is that of *contradiction*. When writing a report it is rather easy to be speaking of certain observations or test results and then in the very next sentence or paragraph say the opposite. If there is conflicting information within the client's record, be sure to point this out so that your reader will not interpret this as *your* error. Most important of all, do not logically build up a picture of your client within the body of the report and then present a diagnosis which is *totally irrelevant to the supportive data.* Base the diagnosis on *what you present* in the report. Also, avoid the practice of lengthy reports. There are few circumstances where one would write more than five or six pages (excluding test profile sheets, answer sheets, etc.) on a given client. You are not to write a book on the client or patient each time you evaluate him.

If there is time, first make a rough draft of your report. Then, read the report to check on the language, grammar, style, communicative ability, and continuity of thought. Any necessary corrections should then be made. The report should also be analyzed as to whether or not it leads to the diagnosis you have made. Then, put the report aside. Later, retrieve the report and give it another reading. You will probably be amazed at some glaring errors which you seemed to have overlooked on the first reading. Correct the draft again. If you are satisfied with its content, then have it typed; if not, lay it aside once more and then reread it at a later time.

If you do not have an experienced person to type your reports, you should instruct your secretary to type your materials *exactly* as you have written them. Any number of otherwise good reports have been abused by being erroneously typed. This is especially true when quoting your client's statements *ad verbum.* Your secretary should not correct a client's grammar or speech idiosyncrasies, nor should she "fill in" gaps in the client's thoughts. These "gaps" usually have highly significant clinical meaning.

When having your report typed you should always have a copy made for your records. This extra copy can be very useful when making follow-up reports and for checking your patient's therapeutic progress. You should have a personal copy even if a copy is retained in your departmental files as much time can be saved by having a readily accessible copy.

One of the more effective ways to learn the mechanics of writing a report is to write one. In the final analysis, "the proof of the pudding is in the eating," or *writing* as our case may be. Until you have experienced the procedure involved in writing a report it will have limited meaning for you. At first, you may feel that it takes an exceptionally long time to prepare a report. In fact, you may feel that you are constantly referring to your reference texts and the test materials in order to decide upon a diagnosis or a course of treatment to prescribe. But, with the completion of each report the next one will come a little easier and will be written more quickly. Do not be discouraged if you spend several hours in writing your first report. After you have written several, you will probably find that you can compose a six or seven page report in an hour or so.

Effective ways of viewing your raw data and of organizing the information will come with practice. The more reports you prepare the more knowledgeable of psychological conditions and behavioral configurations you will become. In fact, the writing of psychological reports will tend to sharpen your diagnostic skills which will ultimately aid you in conducting psychiatric examinations.

Let's write that report!

BIBLIOGRAPHY

Alexander, F. G., and Selesnick, S. T.: *The History of Psychiatry*. New York, Harper & Row, 1966.

American Personnel and Guidance Association: *Ethical Standards*. Washington, D. C., APGA, 1961.

American Psychiatric Association: *Diagnostic and Statistical Manual of Mental Disorders: I*. Washington, D. C.: APA, 1952.

American Psychiatric Association: *Diagnostic and Statistical Manual of Mental Disorders: II*. Washington, D. C.: APA, 1968.

Cheney, D. L. Program analysis at Colorado State. *SK & F Psychiat Rep*, 34:3-5, 1967.

City and County of San Francisco vs. Superior Court, 37 Cal 2d 227 (1951).

Crowley, J. F.: Information processing for mental hosptials: Paper presented at the 8th IBM Medical Symposium at Poughkeepsie, New York, April 3-6, 1967.

Data Processing Magazine. (December), p. 10, 1967.

Durham vs. United States, 214 F. 2d 862 (D. C. Cir, 1954).

Eiduson, B. T.; Brooks, S. H., and Motto, R. L.: Computers in behavioral science. *Behav Sci*, 11:133-142, 1966.

Fitzgibbon, T. J.: The ethical and legal position of the counselor in divulging test information. *Meas Eval Guid*, 1:6-15, 1968.

Foster, A.: Writing psychological reports. *J Clin Psychol*, 7:195, 1951.

Garfield, S. L.; Heine, R. W., and Leventhal, M.: An evaluation of psychological reports in a clinical setting. *J Consult Psychol*, 18:281-286, 1954.

Glueck, B. C.: Computers in psychiatry. *Amer J Psychiat*, 122:325-326, 1965a.

Glueck, B. C. The use of computers in patient care. *Hosp Community Psychiat*, 16:117-120, 1965b.

Graetz, R. E. The computer: A new tool for psychiatry. *Hosp Community Psychiat*, 17:66-73, 1966.

Grold, L. J. Problems of confidentiality in treating adolescents. *Hosp Community Psychiat*, 19:30-31, 1968.

Guttmacher, M. S., and Weihofen, H. *Psychiatry and the Law*. New York, Norton, 1952.

Hammond, K. R., and Allen, J. M., Jr. *Writing Clinical Reports*. New York, Prentice-Hall, 1953.

Hildreth, J .D.: Legislative Consultant, American Psychological Association. Personal communication, June 12, 1968.

Hoch, E. L., and Darley, J. G. A case at law. *Amer Psychol*, 17:623-654, 1962.

Honeywell Corporation: *Fundamentals of Electronic Data Processing*. Wellesley Hills, Mass., Honeywell, 1964.

Huber, J. T.: *Report Writing in Psychology and Psychiatry*. New York, Harper, 1961.

Jenkins vs. United States. 307 F. 2d 637 (D.C. Cir. 1962).

Klopfer, W. G.: *The Psychological Report*. New York, Grune & Stratton, 1960.

Lodge, G. T.: How to write a psychological report. *J Clin Psychol*, 9:400-402, 1953.

Louisell, D. W.: The psychologist in today's legal world. *Minn Law Rev*, 39:235-272, 1955.

Louisell, D. W. The psychologist in today's legal world: Part II. *Minn Law Rev*, 41:731-750, 1957.

Martin, W. T.: *Guidelines for Writing Psychological Reports*. Jacksonville, Ill.: Psychologists and Educators Press, 1970, 8 Pp.

Morgan vs. State, Fla App (1962).

Morrow, R. S.: The diagnostic psychological report. *Psychiat Quart Suppl*, 28:102-110, 1954.

Noyes, A. P., and Kolb, L. C.: *Modern Clinical Psychiatry*. Philadelphia: Lippincott, 1963.

People vs. Hawthorne, 293 Mich 15, 291 N W 205 (1940).

Pia, A. G.: From analytic engine to computer systems. *Hospitals*, 38:1-4, 1964.

Prakken, S. L. (Ed.): *Subject Guide to Books in Print*. New York, Bowker, 1967.

Robitscher, J. B.: *Pursuit of Agreement: Psychiatry and the Law*. Philadelphia, Lippincott, 1966.

Rosenberg, M., and Carriker, D.: Automated nursing notes. *Amer J Nurs*, 66:1966 (Reprint).

Rosenberg, M.; Glueck, B. C., and Bennett, W. L.: Automation of behavioral observations on hospitalized psychiatric patients. *Amer J Psychiat*, 123:926-929, 1967.

Rosenberg, M.; Glueck, B. C., and Stroebel, C. F.: The computer and the clinical decision process. *Amer J Psychiat*, 124:595-599, 1967.

Scott, P. D.: Psychiatric reports for magistrate's courts. *Brit J Delinq*, 4:82-97, 1953.

Sloesbee vs. Balkcom, 339 US 9 (1950).

Slovenko, R.: *Psychotherapy, Confidentiality, and Privileged Communication*. Springfield, Ill., Thomas, 1966.

Smith vs. United States, 350 US 1 (1959).

Spitzer, R. L., and Wilson, P. T.: A guide to the American Psychiatric Association's new diagnostic nomenclature. *Amer J Psychiat, 124*:1619-1629, 1968.
Starkweather, J. A.: Computer simulation of psychiatric interviewing. In Kline, N. S. and Laska, E. (Eds.) *Computers and Electronic Devices in Psychiatry.* New York, Grune & Stratton, 1968.
State vs. Tull. 240 Md. 49, 212 A.2d 729 (1965).
Sullivan, H. S.: *The Psychiatric Interview.* New York, Norton, 1954.
Tallent, N., and Reiss, W. J.: Multidisciplinary views on the preparation of written clinical psychological reports. I:Spontaneous suggestions for content. *J Clin Psychol, 15*:218-221, 1959.
Taylor vs. United States, 18 USC, 4244 (1951).
Thorne, F. C.: A new outline for psychological report writing. *J Clin Psychol, 12*:115-122, 1956.
United States vs. Chrisos, 291 F 2d, 535 (7th Cir, 1961).
Williams vs. New York, 337 US 241 (1948).

Appendix

SUGGESTED READING LIST IN COMPUTER SCIENCE

Books

Kleinmuntz, B.: *Personality Measurement.* Homewood, Ill., Dorsey Press, 1967.

Kline, N. S., and Laska, E. (Eds.): *Computers and other Electronic Devices in Psychiatry.* New York, Grune & Stratton, 1968.

Stacy, R. W., and Waxman, B. D. (Eds.): *Computers in Biomedical Research.* New York, Academic Press, 1965.

Articles

Applying computer procedures to hospital psychiatry, *Roche Rep: Frontiers of Hosp Psychiat* (Oct., 1966), 19-20.

Colby, K. M.: Computer simulation of change in personal belief systems. *Behav Sci,* 12:3, 248-253, 1967.

Colby, K. M., and Gilbert, J. P.: Programming a computer model of neurosis. *J Math Psychol,* 1:405-417, 1964.

Fitzgerald, R. V.: System design for behavioral observation reporting. Proceedings of the 7th IBM Medical Symposium, 1965.

Gravity, M. A., *et al.*: Procedures and problems in computer analysis of the MMPI. *J Psychol,* November, 1965.

Overall, J. E., *et al.*: Computer procedures for psychiatric classification. *JAMA,* February, 1963.

Rome, H. P.: Symposium on automation techniques in personality assessment. Proceedings of the Mayo Clinic, January, 1962.

Technical Manuals

Honeywell Corporation: *Fundamentals of Electronic Data Processing.* Wellesley Hills, Mass., Honeywell Corporation, 1964.

IBM Corporation: *Clinical and Administrative Record System: Information Processing for the Mental Hospital.* New York, IBM Corporation, 1967.

IBM Corporation: *Computer Techniques in Patient Use at the Institute of Living.* New York, IBM Corporation, n.d.

IBM Corporation: *General Information Manual: Introduction to IBM Data Processing Systems.* New York, IBM Corporation, 1964.

IBM Corporation: *System/360 at Rockland State Hospital.* New York, IBM Corporation, n.d.

Professional Journals

Data Management	Journal of Data Management 505 Busse Highway Park Ridge, Illinois 60068
Data Processing Magazine	Data Processing Magazine 134 North Thirteenth St. Philadelphia, Pennsylvania 19107
Information Processing Journal	Cambridge Communications Corporation 1612 K-Street, N. W. Washington, D. C. 20006
Software Age	Software Age Magazine 1020 Church St. Evanston, Illinois 60201
Systems and Procedures Journal	Systems and Procedures Association 24587 Bagley Rd. Cleveland, Ohio 44138

Data Banks and Research Organizations

American Institutes for Research
   8555 Sixteenth Street
   Silver Spring, Maryland 20910

135 North Bellefield Avenue
Pittsburgh, Pennsylvania 15213

PO Box 1113
Palo Alto, California 94302

Note: The reader can obtain additional information from the Library of Congress, Washington, D. C., and from other Federal agencies on Federal and private agencies.

Computer Test Service, Time-Sharing, and Consulting

Harcourt, Brace, & World, Inc.
Test Department
757 Third Avenue
New York, New York 10017

Management Scientists, Inc.
101 Park Avenue
Department SA8-68
New York, New York 10017

National Computer Systems
1015 South 6th Street
Minneapolis, Minn. 55415

Psychodynamics Research Testing Co.
4241 Maple
Dearborn, Michigan 48126

Psychologists and Educators, Inc.*
Suite 212
211 West State St.
Jacksonville, Ill. 62650

Sargent and Lundy Engineers
140 So. Dearborn Street
Chicago, Illinois 60603

Science Research Associates, Inc.
259 East Erie Street
Chicago, Illinois 60611

Testing and Advisement Service
8 Hamilton Terrace
Upper Montclair, New Jersey 07043

The Psychological Corporation
Statistical and Research Division
304 East 45th Street
New York, New York 10017

Computer Hardware and Software Manufacturers

Automata Corporation
1305 Mansfield Avenue
Richland, Washington 99352

Bendix Corporation
Fisher Building
Detroit, Michigan 48202

---

*Consulting services in program evaluation, research, test development, and non-computer systems development only.

Control Data Corporation
8100-34th Avenue, South
Minneapolis, Minnesota 55440

Honeywell Corporation
Electronic Data Processing Division
60 Walnut Street
Wellesley Hills, Massachusetts 02181

IBM Corporation
112 E. Post Road
White Plains, New York 10601

National Cash Register Company
Electronics Division
2873 West El Segundo Blvd.
Hawthorne, California 90250

Optical Scanning Corporation
PO Box 40
Newtown, Pennsylvania 18940

RCA
Information Systems Division
Camden, New Jersey 08010

Sperry Rand Corporation (Univac)
1290 Avenue of the Americas
New York, New York 10019

INDEX

A

Abbreviations, use of, 28, 33
Absolutism, in reports, 26-28
Alexander and Selesnick, 158
Ambiguity in writing, 26
American Psychiatric Association, 42-46
Amicus curiae, 152
Ammons FRPV Test, 77, 102
Ammons Quick Test, 115
Analog system, 118, *see also* Computers
APA codes, 42-46, 139
APA Diagnostic Manual, 43-46
A Priori relationships, 155
Audience, reading, 7

B

Behavioral factors, 11, 65
Behavior modification, 46
Bender Visual-Motor Gestalt Test, 28-29, 115
Binet Scales, 73
BVMG Test, 28

C

Camarillo Hospital Project, 123
Case studies, 55, 56, 67-72, 75-79 81-89, 91-98, 100-106, 108-116.
Church confessional, 147
Civil rights of patients, 156-159, 152-153
Clinical psychologists, 3, 30-39
Coherence in reports, 23 ff.
Colorado Hospital Project, 124-125
Communication, 6, 148-149, 170
Comprehensive psychological, 10, 36, 99-117
Computers in reports, 118-146
Computers, actual reports, 125-142
Computers, history, 118-120
Computers, mental health projects, 122-125

Computers, psychological uses, 120-122
Cumulative record notes, 32
Confidentiality, 6, 147
Consent of release forms, 160-169
Conservators, 157
Content of the report, 5, 10-13
Continued hospitalization reports, 38-39
Contradictions in writing, 170-171
Cooperative English Test, 100, 104
CPI Test, 28
Costs of computerization, 143-146
Counseling interview summary, 31
Counselors, 30-39
Court cases, 149, 151-153, 158-159
Court evaluations, 38, 147-169

D

Daniel M'Naghten, 158
Data bank storage, 166-167
Descriptive writing, 24
Developmental history, 62, 135-138
Diagnosis, 12, 40-51
Diagnosis, primary and secondary, 46-47
Diagnostic and statistical manual, 42-46
Diagnostic impression, 47-48
Diagnostic nomenclature (APA), 42-46
Diagnostic models, 41-47
Diagnostic summary statement, 50-51
Differential aptitude tests, 100
Digital computer, 118
Discharge notes, 39
Dogmatic statements, use of, 26
Domitius Ulpianus, 158
Dialog in reports, use of, 81-87
Disease *vs.* defect concept in court, 151-152, 158
Durham Rule in court, 151

E
EEG, 114
Eiduson, *et al.*, 125
Einstein, A., 23
Electroencephalogram, 114
Elipses, use of in reports, 15
Emotional factors, 11, 64
Ethical standards, APGA, 147, 154
Evidence, legal, 60, 154
Expert witnesses, testimony of, 38, 60, 150-152, 155-156, 168.
Extraneous material in reports, 28-29

F
Facts in reports, 154
FBI, 160
Federal agencies, 160
Fifth amendment, 153, 156
Final diagnosis, 40-51
First-hand information, 6
Fitzgibbon, T. J., 162
Forensic psychology, 38, 44, 147-169
Format of reports, 14-22
Foster, A., 3
Freud, S., 150
FSIQ, 28

G
Garfield, S. L., 3
GIGO, 120, *see also* Computers
Goodenough Draw-A-Man Test, 77, 79
Gorham Proverbs Test, 100, 104
Graetz, R. E., 124
Graham-Kendall MFD Test, 28, 110
Grammatical tense, in writing, 15, 23-29, 171
Grold, L. J., 153, 162
Group psychotherapy notes, 37
Guilford-Zimmerman Test, 100, 104
Guttmacher & Weihofen, 155

H
Hammond and Allen, 3
Henry de Bracton, 158
Hildreth, J., 151
Hippocratic Oath, 148
Hoch and Darley, 152
Hollerith Code, 118, *see also* Computers

Honeywell Corporation, 119
Huber, J. T., 3

I
IBM 360 computer, 121
Identifying data, 62
Impression, diagnostic, 40-51
Incompetence, legal, 156-157
Inferences in report writing, 19
Institute of living project, 123
Intellectual evaluation, 9, 73-80
Intellectual factors, 64
Interview data and notes, 8, 11, 36-37
I.Q., 28, 33

J
Jargon, psychological, 108
Jenkins *vs* United States, 152

K
Klopfer, W. G., 3
Kuder Preference Record, 100

L
Lamartine, A., 23
Language of the report, 23-29, 171
Legal aspects in writing, 38, 58-60, 147-169
Legal release forms, 160-169
Levels, diagnostic, 47-51
Licensure of psychologists, 150-151
Lodge, G. T., 3
Louisell, D. W., 153

M
Manual, APA diagnostic, 43-46
MAPS Test, 81-87
Medical records releases, 160-169
Mental competency, 156-159
Mental status, 59, 63
Mental Status Exam, 127-134, *see also* Computers
Minnesota-Hartford Test, 123
Minors and the courts, 163
MMPI computerized reports, 123
MMPI Test, 88-89, 104, 107, 111, 145
M'Naghten Rule, 158
Models, diagnostic, 40 ff.
Model penal code, 158

Morgan *vs* State, 159
Morrow, R. S., 3-4
MQ, 28
Multiple diagnoses, 40-51

N

NCR answer sheet, 134, 139-141
Neurological findings, 29, 114
"Newspeak," 23
Noyes and Klob, 61, 154

O

Observation skills, 58
Optical scan forms, 122, *see also* Computers
Organization of reports, 14-22, 172
Orwell, G., 23
Outlines for reports, 14-22

P

Patient confidentiality, 147-169
People *vs* Hawthorne, 152
Physical history, 62
Pia, A. G., 118
Post facto reports, 58-59
Prakken, S. L., 3
Pre-admission status, 55
Preciseness in writing, 26
Pre-sentencing reports, 159-160
Priests, 147
Primary readers, 7
Privileged communication, 148-149, 153
Procedures, diagnostic, 40-42
Prognosis, 12
Progress notes, 9, 37-38
PsyCHES system, 118-146, *see also* Computers
Psychiatric examination, 57-72
Psychiatric examination, cases, 67-72
Psychiatrists, 150-152
Psychological evaluations, 31-32
Psychological exams, comprehensive, 10, 36, 99-117
Psychological exams, intellectual, 75-80
Psychological exams, personality, 81-90
Psychological jargon, use of, 108
Psychologists and reports, 3, 30-39
Psychometrists, 3

Psychotherapy reports, 36-37
Punched Cards, 122, *see also* Computers
Purpose of reports, 5

Q

QT, 28
Qualifying phrases, use of, 46-47
Quantitative terms, use of, 25

R

Railroad Retirement Administration, 160
Random Access Storate, 123, *see also* Computers
Reasons for evaluation, 11
Recommendations in reports, use of, 12
Records, 153-155
Referral reports, 32
Reiss-Davis project, 125
Release forms, 160-169
Reports in general, 30-39
Reports to parents, 33-34
Reports to teachers, 33
Research Laboratory Data Sheet, 139-142
Robitscher, J. B., 157
Rockland State Hospital Project, 124
Rosenberg, *et al.*, 124

S

San Francisco *vs* superior court, 149
Sanity hearings, 156-159
SCAT Tests, 100, 104
School counseling reports, 100-107
Screening evaluations, 9
Screening of patients, 35
Scott, P. D., 4
SCRIBE system, 124, *see also* Computers
Secondary readers, 7
Sequential access, 123, *see also* Computers
Sloesbee *vs* balkcom, 159
Slovenko, R., 148, 150, 153, 154-156.
Smith *vs* United States, 159
Social behavior factors, 65-66
Social History Statement, 8, 10, 52-55
Social Security Administration, 160

Specialized terms, use of, 25
Spitzer and Wilson, 44
SQ, 28
Staffing reports, 35-36
Starkweather, J. A., 126
State agencies, 161
State laws, variance in, 35, 150
State *vs* Tull, 152
Style, writing, 8
Sullivan, H. S., 58, 60
Summary statements, use of, 11
Superfluousness in report writing, 28-29
System progress note, 134, *see also* Computers

T

Tallent and Reiss, 3
TAT, 28
Taylor *vs* United States, 153
Teleprocessing, 122, *see also* Computers
Tennessee Self Concept Scale, 88-89
Tense, grammatical, 15
Tentative diagnosis, 40-51

Terms, coining of, 24
Theragnostic report, 93-98
Therapy progress report, 91-98
Thorne, F. C., 3
Time-Sharing, 144, *see also* Computers
Treatment program reports, 36, 91-98
Treatment summary reports, 9, 10, 91-98
Types of reports, 8-10

U

United States *vs* Chrisos, 159
United States Secret Service, 160

V

Verbatim Reports, use of, 81-87, 94-98, 171
Veteran's Administration, 160

W

WAIS, 28, 75, 94, 100, 104, 110, 115.
Watson-Glazer CTA Test, 100
Wechsler Scales, *see* WAIS, WISC
Williams *vs* New York, 159
WISC, 77, 102